# THE AMERICAN HOUSE

100 Contemporary Homes

# HOUSE

Published in Australia in 2017 by
The Images Publishing Group Pty Ltd
ABN 89 059 734 431
6 Bastow Place, Mulgrave, Victoria 3170, Australia
Tel: +61 3 9561 5544  Fax: +61 3 9561 4860
books@imagespublishing.com
www.imagespublishing.com

Copyright © The Images Publishing Group Pty Ltd 2017
The Images Publishing Group Reference Number: 1364

All renderings, plans, and illustrations have been supplied courtesy of the
architect; photography is attributed throughout, unless otherwise noted.
Pages 10–11: © Joshua McHugh, Ferry Road

National Library of Australia Cataloguing-in-Publication entry:

Title:      The American House: 100 contemporary homes
ISBN:       9781864707380 (hardback)
Subjects:   Architecture, Domestic—United States.
            Architectural design—United States.
            Architecture, Modern—21st century.

Group art director/production manager: Nicole Boehringer
Research contributors: Joe Boschetti, Andrea Monfried
Senior editor: Gina Tsarouhas
Coordinating editor: Hannah Jenkins
Graphic designer: Ryan Marshall

Printed on 140gsm GoldEast Matt Art paper by Everbest Printing Investment
Limited, in Hong Kong/China

IMAGES has included on its website a page for special notices in relation to this
and our other publications. Please visit www.imagespublishing.com

Introduction by Ian Volner

# THE AMERICAN

100 Contemporary Homes

# HOUSE

Edited by Hannah Jenkins

images
Publishing

# CONTENTS

# INTRODUCTION by Ian Volner

Ever since critic Kenneth Frampton (quoting philosopher Paul Ricœur) declared that architecture should find a way both 'to become modern and to return to sources,' progressive designers the world over have taken to reexamining every aspect of their local building traditions, local culture, and local climate, looking to temper their contemporaneity with—dare one say it?—*authenticity*. 'Critical regionalism,' as Frampton termed it in his famed 1983 essay, is now a worldwide phenomenon, and nowhere is its presence so pervasive than in the field of housing. This most fundamental unit of architecture is also a convenient typological testing ground for a flexible architectural language, one whose particular vocabulary varies from place to place and moment to moment, but whose basic syntax remains universal and of our time.

So what happens to a nominally critical architecture when it turns into a normative mode of practice? Well, a lot of things. Chronicled in this book is the residential work of a wide range of practices, from international headliners to thriving local studios, all of whom share a sort of contrapuntal relationship to the basic technics and aesthetics of mainstream modern design. Each studio weaves back and forth—each to their own degree—between, on the one hand, a baseline obligation to spatial and geometric essentials, and on the other the specifics of the particular site and client, achieving a synthesis that's never quite off-the-shelf, never quite a one-off. What one discovers is that the American house in the 21st century has become the repository of a regionalism so refined, so adaptable, and so porous that it's almost impossible to define as regionalism per se, much less as critical. There is scarcely any mainstream to be critical of anymore, as a thousand flowers bloom and themes from different eras and areas commingle with dizzying abandon.

Ian Volner is a writer and critic, and has contributed articles on design, urbanism, and architecture to *The Wall Street Journal*, *Harper's*, *The New Republic*, and *The New Yorker* online, among other publications. His most recent book, *This Is Frank Lloyd Wright*, was a winner of the DAM Book Award from the Frankfurt Book Fair and named one of the ten-best design titles of 2016; his next book is a biography of architect Michael Graves (Princeton Architectural Press). He lives in Manhattan.

That the house should be the vehicle of such diversity in the United States is surprisingly only to the extent that, until fairly lately, uniformity was the order of the day in domestic residential construction. From the advent of the balloon frame in the 19th-century, American homes marched more or less in lockstep with passing stylistic fads and with each other, creating whole neighborhoods of Queen Anne and Tudor interspersed with the odd Prairie School. The automation and mass suburbanization that followed the conclusion of the Second World War didn't so much change that pattern as supercharge it, as hordes of Cape Cods and ranch houses overran the landscape at a breakneck pace. Even into the present century, single-family residential development has largely been the province of the exurban real-estate developers and their oversized McMansions, hypertrophied versions of the Cold War ramblers that preceded them. But within this, this sea of sameness, there have arisen a few islands of originality, and slowly, bit by bit, they have now grown into a vast archipelago.

The most striking aspect of this phenomenon, visible at once in these pages, isn't merely the disparate approaches evident *between* projects. Obviously many miles and a much different sensibility separate, say, the 50 Oakwood house of Stanley Saitowitz | Natoma Architects in San Franicso—an exquisite exercise in urban asceticism— from Cutler Anderson Architects' Beaux Arts House in Seattle—a gratifyingly textural specimen of old-fashioned organicism. What's more arresting is the layered variety of sources and impulses identifiable *within* each project. In Barnes Coy's Beach House in East Quogue, New York, the late Charles Gwathmey's sculptural exterior effects collide with his old friend Richard Meier's spatial theatrics, with just a little bit of Norman Jaffe's romanticism thrown in for good measure. In Searl Lamaster Howe's Asbury Residence, Italian Rationalism collides with Art Deco collides with Danish Modern interior accents, all of it plopped down improbably in Evanston, Illionis. Art House 2.0, from Carol Kurth Architecture, adopts a rustic look appropriate to its setting in Westchester, New York, but that specifically recalls the early houses of Philip Johnson, making it a cleverly derivative take on another cleverly derivative architect.

The controlling forces of homebuilding in the United States today—chief among them ecological sensitivity and regulatory measures—have been so thoroughly digested by the architectural profession that they impose but few limits on designers' formal imagination. With so much possibility before them, it's the more wonder that restraint remains such a touchstone for designers of high-end designer housing. The ones shown here seem to be kept in check, not by dedication to a single overarching philosophy (even one so capacious as regionalism), but simply by good taste, which they have in abundance and appear intent on spreading from sea to shining sea.

9

# 100 Contemporary Homes

*... from sea to shining sea*

This renovation draws upon the formal logic imbedded in an original structure to create a contemporary home for a family of four. The original home, built in the 1980s, contained tall, day-lit volumes but was worn, tired, and needed attention. The owners, having lived in the house for eight years prior to renovation, were accustomed to the home's strengths and weaknesses. Particularly fond of the location, they wanted to take advantage of the surrounding setting by improving visual connection to the landscape. They also desired additional space for entertaining and a more open interior.

To accomplish these goals the original home's formal logic was identified. This analysis suggested a massing strategy in which a simple gabled volume could be 'sliced' into three sections and offset from one another to create a stepped façade facing the woods. This simple strategy was compromised at the entry and garage, rendering it virtually illegible. In addition, many of the interior volumes, while lofty, were subdivided with partitions, creating a warren of rooms rather than open flowing spaces.

Substance Architecture

# 3LP RESIDENCE

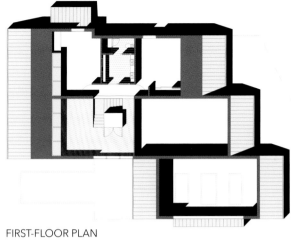

FIRST-FLOOR PLAN

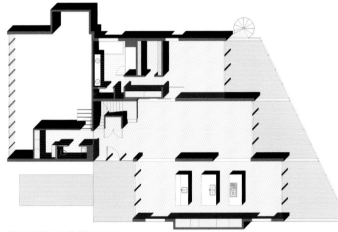

GROUND-FLOOR PLAN

Location **Iowa City, Iowa** Area **4725 ft² (439 m²)** Completed **2015** Photography **Paul Crosby**

The renovation drew upon this original organization. The three 'slices' (eating, living, sleeping) implicit in the existing home were reinforced. The angled wall at the entry was straightened and realigned to clarify the plan. Interior partitions separating the dining space from the kitchen and living spaces were removed to create large, open volumes. The stair was relocated to open up the living area, and the thresholds between slices were delineated. Wall-to-wall operable openings were placed at the ends of the 'slices' to connect the airy, day-lit interior to the wooded site and enhance the sense of entry from the street. Finally, a large deck was created to unify the rear elevation and provide space for exterior entertaining.

While the renovation added less than 300 square feet (28 square meters), the visual impact is immense. Thoroughly transformed, this project takes full advantage of the home's site, interior volume, and daylight to create a unique and contemporary home.

Built for a couple with children from previous marriages, this home's design objective focused on bridging two families together within a livable piece of art. It is an experiment in transparency and solid form; removing borders and edges between inside and outside to depict flowing and endless space.

The floor plan was derived by pushing and pulling the structural form to maximize the backyard and minimize the public front yard, while welcoming the sun in key rooms by rotating the house 45-degrees to true north. This angular form is a result of the family's program, zoning rules, lot attributes, and the sun's path. The architect wanted to construct a house that was engineered to be smart and efficient. One that not only looked modern but also acted modern, with every aspect of user control simplified to a digital touch button. A planning module, based on an interstitial connecter, was developed to keep hallways, bathrooms, stairs, and mechanical areas uncluttered and pure. A large formal foyer celebrates the home's entry and opens up to the living, dining, kitchen, and family rooms, which all focus on the rear garden. On the east side of the second floor is the master wing, with a center bridge connecting it to the children's wing on the west.

Thomas Roszak Architecture

# 7RR ECO-HOME

The home's wood frame, with steel beams used for longer spans, allowed the design brief to be realized both architecturally and from a budget standpoint. This timeless, high quality, and sustainable home provides the family with a positive and unified residential experience.

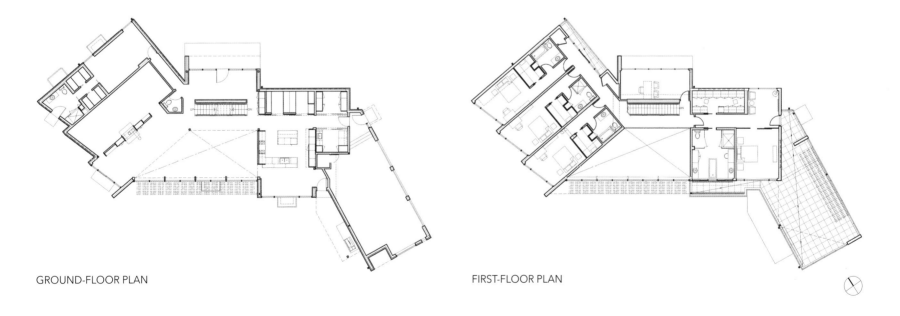

GROUND-FLOOR PLAN

FIRST-FLOOR PLAN

Location **Northfield, Illinois** Area **6200 ft² (576 m²)** Completed **2013** Photography **Scott McDonald, Hedrich Blessing**

The site's existing home, built in 1926, was in a state of neglect and decay. Originally set back from the street, the reconstruction of the home included the addition of a new contemporary façade of white concrete, with large punched openings added to extend to the front property line.

The house was expanded at the rear and two new floors were added. On the ground floor is a garage and one-bedroom apartment, which expands into a sunken garden that steps up into the rear yard. A central stair provides access to the unit above. This core divides the plan into front rooms, which face the street and garden rooms opening to the yard. A central light well matches the light well of the neighboring house and illuminates this center. Stretching from the light well in the living room is a long floating fireplace.

On the street, this new building complements the scale of surrounding houses, with a central bay flanked by smaller bays on the property lines. The chalky white concrete frame supports large areas of glazing made possible by contemporary construction, but retains the simple material palette, mass, and color that typifies so many of San Francisco's residential buildings.

Stanley Saitowitz | Natoma Architects Inc.

# 50 OAKWOOD

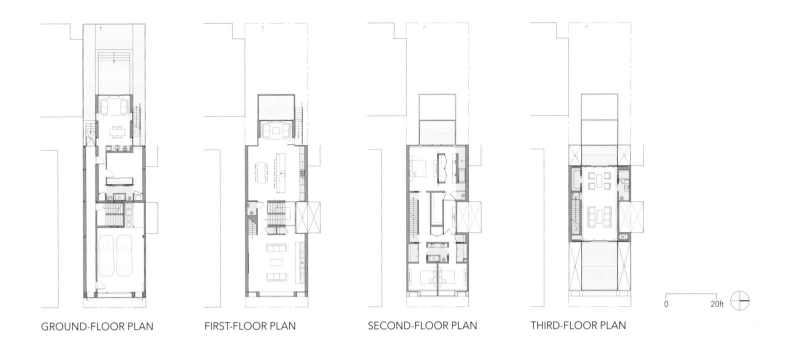

GROUND-FLOOR PLAN     FIRST-FLOOR PLAN     SECOND-FLOOR PLAN     THIRD-FLOOR PLAN

0     20ft

The kitchen stretches from the light well to the rear, with dining and a sitting area opening to a terrace. Above is the master suite, again opening onto a terrace in the rear, with two bedrooms at the front. At the top, a single large room is an open frame to both front and rear, with views from downtown to the hills opening to terraces on both sides.

Location **San Francisco, California** Area **5300 ft² (492 m²)** Completed **2016** Photography **Bruce Damonte**

The 510 House is a private residence located in a postwar suburb on Milwaukee's North Shore, its volume carefully embedded in the site's gently sloping contours and cradled by the mature trees and thick underbrush lining the property's edges. The owners, a professional couple with busy work schedules, asked for a house that would accommodate their conflicting desires for privacy and serenity, and frequent hosting of social events.

In response, the home's program was organized as two interlocking building forms, their 'T' configuration bifurcating the site into a public entry court for visitors and vehicles, and a private, visually shielded green space in the back. Parking, service functions, and the master suite are consolidated in a long, single-story bar: a narrow, wood-clad volume that straddles the two sides of the property along its western edge. Spaces for guests and entertainment are housed in a perpendicular volume defined by a continuous concrete block ribbon.

Johnsen Schmaling Architects

# 510 HOUSE

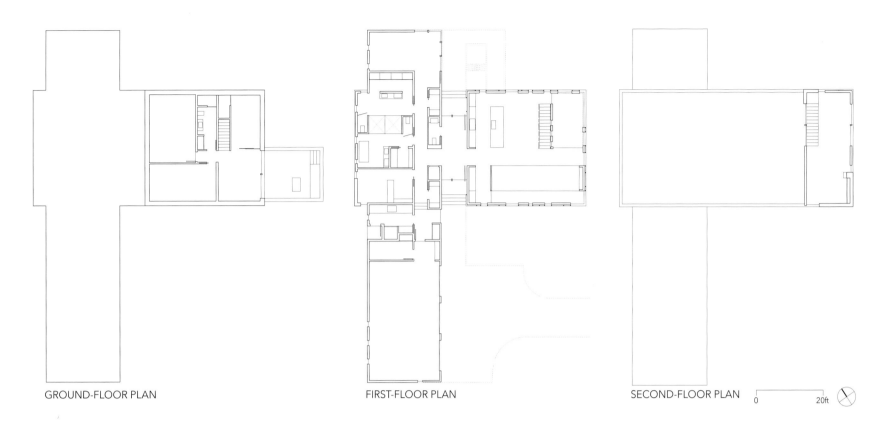

GROUND-FLOOR PLAN                    FIRST-FLOOR PLAN                    SECOND-FLOOR PLAN    0 ___ 20ft

The deeply recessed entry vestibule provides access to both private and public quarters and leads into the adjacent open living hall. The color green serves as an architectural device to infuse the interior year-round with the lush tones of summer's verdant but short-lived greenery surrounding the site. The green perimeter walls extend their interior hues to the exterior, where they express the volume of the living hall as the building's proud *piano nobile*—a distinct and intelligible architectural element suspended within the folding concrete ribbon of the main building mass to formally emphasize the primary activity hub of the house.

An open, linear kitchen runs along one side of the living hall. The pantry wall transforms into a continuous wooden ceiling liner, spatially defining the dining and lounging area Stairs lead up to the observatory, which provides access to an expansive vegetated roof, and down to a small guest suite, which spills out to an intimate sunken terrace with a fire pit.

The carefully restrained exterior material palette was regionally sourced. On the inside, the wall panels, along with the carefully curated artwork throughout the house, add splashes of color to the deliberately neutral interior backdrop of white walls, grey concrete tiles, and bleached white oak.

Location **Milwaukee, Wisconsin** Area **3500 ft² (335 m²)** Completed **2016** Photography **John J. Macaulay**

Nestled amidst natural stone outcroppings and untouched forest, Art House 2.0 is a serene modern retreat showcasing a growing contemporary art collection. The architect and interior designer, who designed the clients' first residence more than 20 years ago, collaborated with them again in a quest to find the ideal parcel of land on which to design a new one-level-living style home for their enjoyment of nature, art, and love of books.

The result is an open and airy, gallery-like home, which frames views of the natural woodland setting. The use of indigenous stone materials and cedar juxtapose the rectilinear forms and glass expanses. The use of shaded horizontal overhangs takes advantage of natural daylight, illuminating the interior and creating a passive solar effect. Geothermal energy systems implemented in the home further the thoughtful response to environmental aspects.

The clients' extensive art collection was a primary consideration in the early stages of the design process, with strategic allocation of space ensuring optimal showcasing.

Carol Kurth Architecture

# ART HOUSE 2.0

Mid-century furnishings from the original home were incorporated into the new design, giving them new life. Sculpture niches, inside and out, were designed to focus views within the home and further enhance the inside/outside gallery environment.

Designed with views framed to nature, the clients enjoy the art of the landscape and an ever-changing display of nature, while living among the permanent collection of art within. Embedded in the woods, the residence is a tranquil canvas for two art lovers.

Location **Pound Ridge, New York** Area **3600 ft² (334 m²)** Completed **2014** Photography **Albert Vecerka/Esto**

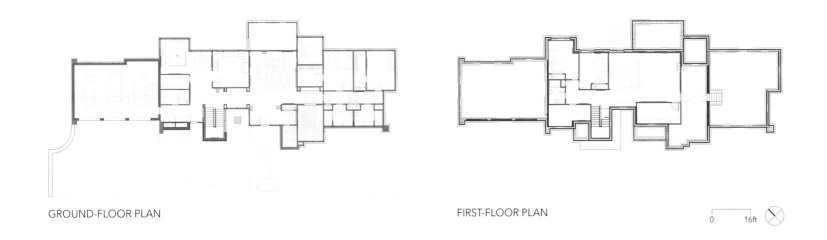

GROUND-FLOOR PLAN

FIRST-FLOOR PLAN

0     16ft

A stately façade not only affords this home prominence within a century-old neighborhood, but also gives it a distinct identity, keeping in accord with the noteworthy eclecticism of surrounding homes. This context granted the architects freedom to pursue the clients' vision for the project—a current-day take on traditional Mediterranean design.

Italian Rationalism of the 1920s, with an emphasis on logic and simplicity, became a launch pad for the home's design. The four-bedroom structure is an amalgam of classic and simple volumes. Detailing throughout is traditional but streamlined, allowing for a focus on volumes of space and how light animates them. Generously scaled windows have been positioned high on walls to bring in light without sacrificing privacy—a key concern given the density of the neighborhood and busy street.

On approaching the house, the classic gable roof disappears from sight and the defining view, instead, becomes a projecting cubic volume. The stucco-clad structure presents a simplistic yet stately street face, contrasting with the informal and private courtyard the home encloses.

Searl Lamaster Howe Architects

# ASBURY RESIDENCE

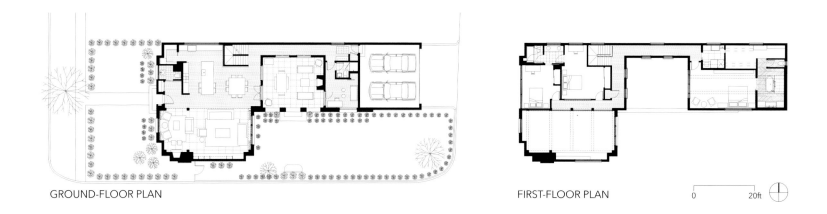

GROUND-FLOOR PLAN

FIRST-FLOOR PLAN

0            20ft

Location **Evanston, Illinois** Area **2800 ft² (260 m²)** Completed **2015** Photography **Tony Soluri**

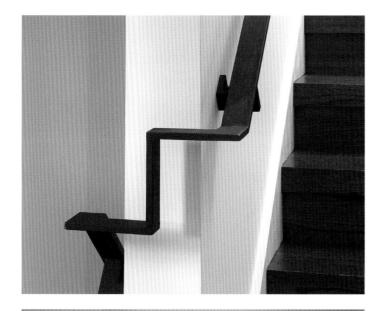

The site once housed a warehouse and effectively was a brownfield requiring extensive soil remediation. The home includes thick walls with extra insulation to minimize energy costs and was built under strict V.O.C (volatile organic compounds) limits. Reused or salvaged materials appear throughout the home and suspended, almost invisible yet highly efficient LED strips discretely illuminate the locally sourced cedar ceiling. Ornamental ironwork dating from the Art Deco period and crafted in Buenos Aires has been repurposed for railings inside and out.

Traditional architectural forms have been reinterpreted to instill a modern spirit in the house, with an end goal of creating a home that is contextually responsive yet clearly of its age. It is a melding of cultures, time periods, materials, and ideas about the definition of space.

After enjoying many summers at the property's existing cottage, built by Robert W. Patterson, the client saw an opportunity for respectful site development and decided to build a four-season guesthouse for his expanding family.

Located on a wooded waterfront site in Bar Harbor, with Blue Hill Mountain in the distance, the surrounding environment is abundant with natural qualities, making preservation of the landscape paramount during construction of the project. The new guesthouse merges seamlessly with the existing landscape and explores new vantage points, boundaries and reciprocity between what is built and what is natural, what is inside and what is outside. Materials were sourced locally and mimic the material choices of the original cottage.

Overlooking the original historic gardens, the new structure is nestled into the hillside by a stone and cedar plinth, which houses a potting shed, garage, and storage. A two-bedroom cottage is set above and sheathed in glass, blackened metal and dark cedar. Furniture has been considered integral to the architecture, with every custom-designed piece tactilely and conceptually engaging with an adjacent architectural surface.

SPAN Architecture

# AUGUST MOON LITTLE HOUSE

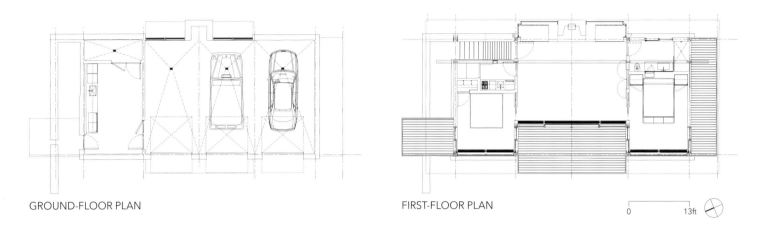

GROUND-FLOOR PLAN

FIRST-FLOOR PLAN

0     13ft

Location **Bar Harbor, Maine** Area **2500 ft² (232 m²)** Completed **2015** Photography **Adrian Gaut**

The ship-lapped interior paneling organizes a variety of functions. The dining table folds down, nestling within the wall to expand the space when not in use. The wall planking that wraps the interior perimeter deforms to provide pulls for the closets, rather than introducing foreign surface knobs. The roof incorporates a wooden sun-shading device facing west.

Drawing from the local vernacular, the guesthouse contributes to the region's existing stock of thoughtful architecture rooted in conservation. In demonstrating a continued commitment to respectful land development and exploring new relationships with the surrounding nature, the guesthouse serves to strengthen its context both at the site and on a regional level.

On the crest of a hill, a white plaster volume floats lazily over a glass-walled living area. Located on the home's main floor, this shaded and airy seam of space enjoys breathtaking views of Los Angeles. With panoramic views spanning across the grid of the Los Angeles basin on one side, and the natural ecosystem of the Hollywood Hills on the other, this home becomes a lens through which to absorb the urban landscape.

Its minimal form—partially a result of its strange and irregular lot—operates at the scale of the mountains. Here, the house takes advantage of its airy position at the top of a hill by introducing a number of design strategies, which use the wind to cool the interior and encourage minimal use of air conditioning, synergistically tying the house to its hillside environment.

Warren Techentin Architecture

# BALCONY HOUSE

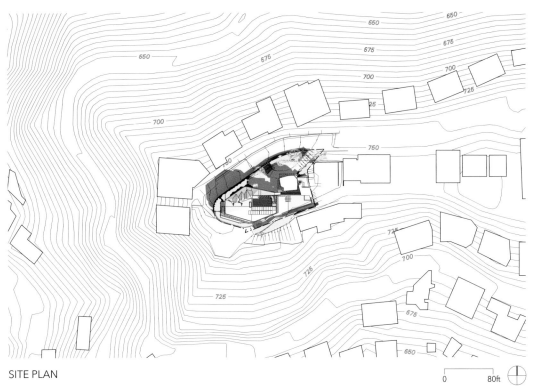

SITE PLAN

0      80ft

The house was designed to embrace strategies of indoor-outdoor living. Embedded in the design are a number of sustainable-living technologies appropriate to its site. Life flows effortlessly between indoor and outdoor rooms as well as shaded and sunny spaces, enabled by huge sliding-glass doors, which open entire rooms to the outdoors. A balcony of varied spatial effects encircles the upper level of the structure and allows a promenade around the house to take in the flora, fauna, and the daily ritual of the weather.

Location **Hollywood Hills, California** Area **4000 ft² (372 m²)** Completed **2016** Photography **Eric Staudenmaier**

This porch-like house sits on a knoll at the corner of two scenic canyons with panoramic views of the city. The living area is raised slightly above the site and faces east, with deep porches on the ground and first floors for outdoor living. Developed as a series of horizontal volumes that merge with the terrain, the exterior deck and landscape merge with the topography to compliment an infinity lap pool at the edge of the canyon hill. The front of the house is distinctly urban and vertical, and includes a floating canopy framing the entry in a garden courtyard. Entering the double-story hall, a threshold redirects attention to the panoramic view through the loft-like living space beyond.

Open-living, dining, and kitchen areas are surrounded by moveable glass doors, which telescope open to the oversized porch and view. A slight shifting of the volumes from the ground floor to the first floor creates large covered exterior areas for dining and lounging.

Griffin Enright Architects

# BARNETT RESIDENCE

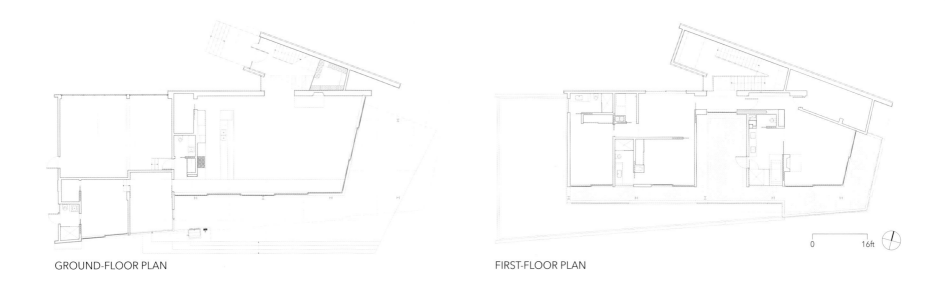

GROUND-FLOOR PLAN

FIRST-FLOOR PLAN

0          16ft

A floating stair arrives at the second-story courtyard and a large opening at the landing of the stair frames a glimpse of the canyon beyond. The master bedroom and its porches float over the outdoor-living room below.

Location **Brentwood, California** Area **4000 ft² (372 m²)** Completed **2014** Photography **Tim Street-Porter**

The replacement of an existing home atop the highest point of an ocean dune encouraged the architects to draw inspiration from a time when cedar beach houses shared an intimate relationship with their unique environment. The defining form of this modern beach cottage is an ellipse with incorporated chiseled curtain walls, which reveal a sweeping view of the ocean to the south. Providing a surprising dynamism, a rectangle sculpted with voids and projections skewers the ellipse and opens to northern bay views. A base of horizontal cedar slats conceals the piles supporting the house above the flood elevation, and gives a sense of enclosure to the carport beneath, another characteristic of the iconic east coast beach houses of the postwar era. Made up of a variety of shapes and forms, this unique art-filled beach house is open, playful, and cozy.

Barnes Coy Architects

# BEACH HOUSE

GROUND-FLOOR PLAN

FIRST-FLOOR PLAN

0   15ft

Location **East Quogue, New York** Area **3200 ft² (397 m²)** Completed **2016** Photography **Paul Domzal/EdgeMediaDigital**

This suburban residence was designed for a family of six on a small lot in a tighlty packed suburban neighborhood. The land, which previously held a small cabin, was blessed with seven magnificent Douglas fir trees in a grassy field. The architects choreographed the circulation of the residence to encourage an emotional connection between the owners and the trees, while maintaining a sense of privacy in a dense, but quiet neighborhood.

The residence itself was organized into two wings, with a central gathering space between them. The west wing houses the children's bedrooms and their playroom. In the east wing are the master suite, study, and guest areas. The central gathering area—containing the kitchen, dining room, and living room—is a single volume defined by a high ceiling and a transparent wall of vertical-lift doors, which open onto the south-facing courtyard. The wooden roof of this central space is supported by four slender steel columns. This high light structure is juxtaposed with the lower, heavy brick wings; a contrasting mass that reinforces the nature of both materials, while viscerally delineating the differences between the public and private zones of the house. With the main axis extending from the front door to the largest of the firs, the trees have become an integral element in the life of the family.

Cutler Anderson Architects

# BEAUX ARTS HOME

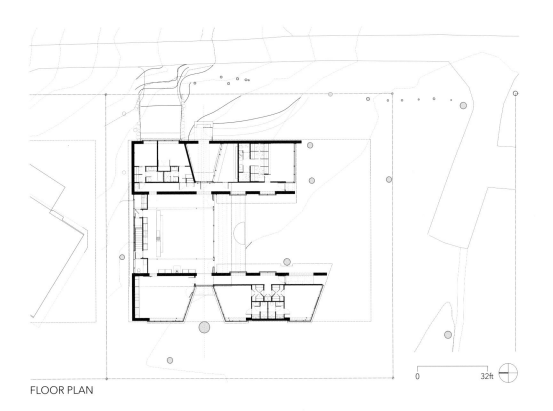

FLOOR PLAN

0                    32ft

An inherent part of the design was the arrangement of high-performance glazing (Cardinal LoĒ²-272) combined with insulation exceeding code requirements to counter the thermal effects of the southern exposure. Radiant heating and energy-efficient appliances further minimize energy usage.

The landscaping is dominated by native vegetation; vine maples, salal, Oregon grape, western swordfern, and native grasses, which are complimented by permeable pavers to reduce runoff. All construction materials, including custom masonry, were locally sourced to further reduce environmental impact.

Location **Seattle, Washington** Area **3850 ft² (358 m²)** Completed **2014** Photography **Benjamin Benschneider**

This Mediterranean Revival project gave new life to an existing and historic home completed in 1930 by Lang & Witchell Architects. The aim was to restore the home to its original intent by expanding and enriching its features.

The home is situated on a large lot and is surrounded by courtyards off of its main rooms. The use of painted brick with headers was not initially appreciated, however, it maintained a sense of age, which was important to honor considering the home had been there for more than 80 years.

Upon entry to the home, along a hedge, there is an enclosed formal garden with square motor court. Parterre front gardens anchor the home and create a ceremonial-like entrance. The building site composition is engaging, with processional brick walkways leading through ornamental trees to a series of small courts, fountain, and entry. Flanked by courtyards, the iconic living room acts as a formal point of welcome to the home.

J. Wilson Fuqua & Associates Architects

# BEVERLY DRIVE

Picturesque details of the original architects work, such as ironwork, balconies, and bays, are highlighted in the intimate entrance courtyard. A 1980s modernist remodel of the home's interior required a major overhaul. An unnecessary hallway was removed to create a major axis from library to stair hall and the staircase. Inspired by Casadel Herrero in Santa Barbara, the reshaped stairs opened the oversized window into the entry. A short vestibule, squeezed under the stairs, separates the entry from the library and gives access to a powder room and wine room via a secret wall panel. The high-gloss library is filled with light from windows facing north to the backyard, and south to a courtyard shaded by an enormous pecan tree. To the right of the entry is a blue and white Portuguese-tile, wainscoted dining room. Designed by Cathy Kincaid, it offers the home the unique aspect of a different time and place.

Location **Dallas, Texas** Area **10,000 ft² (929 m²)** Completed **2015** Photography **Porter Fuqua**

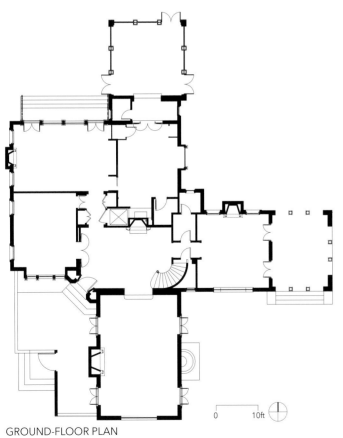

GROUND-FLOOR PLAN

0    10ft

59

The Birch Residence reimagines the typical Los Angeles, postwar tract house to be light filled and open to the entire site. An unexpected and over-scaled curved wall extends through the entry forecourt and runs the length of the home. Above winds a 52-foot (16-meter) skylight along the hall's east-west axis. The curved geometry tracks light from sunrise to sunset. A sunshade of prismatic, polycarbonate panels creates a semi-shaded condition, lighting the interior with diffused reflections and refractions. Translating the sun's movement and intensity, it attenuates delicate shifts in light, creating subtly varying qualities of space and connects the residence to daily and seasonal environment cycles.

Griffin Enright Architects

# BIRCH RESIDENCE

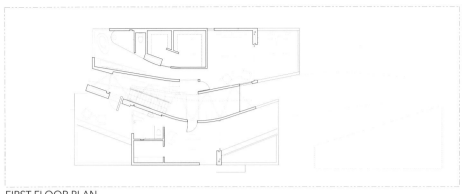

FIRST-FLOOR PLAN

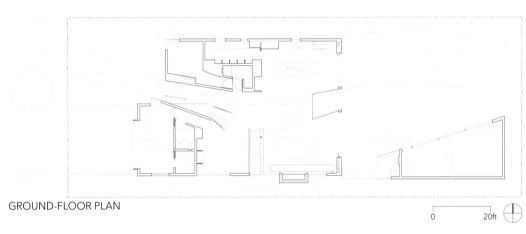

GROUND-FLOOR PLAN

0          20ft

A first-floor glass bridge extends over a sculptural stair, and a narrow pool with a reflective curve reaches into the house and hall through a seamless glass alcove. Movement occurs along the hall's curve, converging and diverging at threshold moments, punctuated by city views. The hall becomes a viewing device for both internal and external connections. Interior volumes expand and transform as the living areas extend outside the home. Although the residence is bisected by the hall and pool, the curved geometry and open ground-floor plan provide visual reconnections through the site, maximizing the apparent interior volume.

Location **Los Angeles, California** Area **3400 ft² (316 m²)** Completed **2015** Photography **Benny Chan/Fotoworks**

The objective of this renovation/addition was to create a modern adaptation, while retaining the iconic gable forms of the existing traditional, lodge-style house.

The floor plan was pushed and pulled to create a sense of compression and release when moving through the spaces. The gable ends have been in-filled completely with glass, allowing natural light and the surrounding aspen grove to permeate inside.

The home's interiors complement the restraint and texture of the exterior materials and form. Handmade artisan furniture and natural materials underscore a mix of modern Italian furniture and fixtures.

Rowland+Broughton

# BLACK BIRCH MODERN

Location **Aspen, Colorado** Area **6400 ft² (595 m²)** Completed **2013** Photography **Brent Hoss Photography, Nick Johnson Photography**

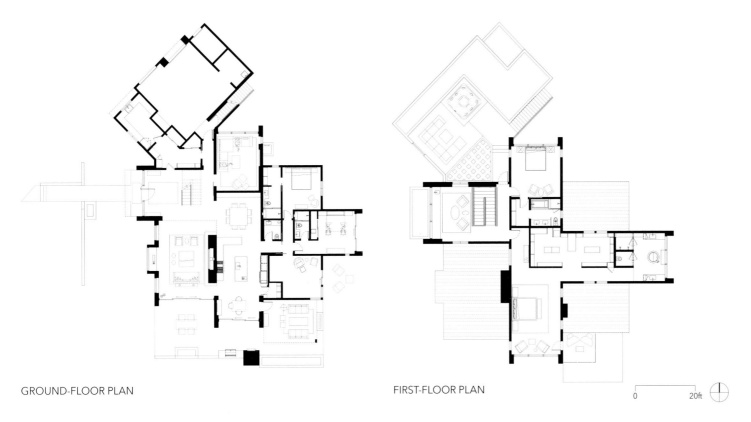

GROUND-FLOOR PLAN
FIRST-FLOOR PLAN

0          20ft

Previously owned by a local architect and renovated several times to include the addition of a two-story steel and glass rear extension, the new owners sought to restore this Brooklyn terrace to its original formality, while adapting it to the modern needs of a growing family.

The structure's detailing had been lost and required some sleuthing in order to achieve the Greek Revival style. In addition to completely reframing the interior, the house also required a new south-facing brick façade due to significant deterioration. The modern extension was replaced with a more traditionally detailed wood and copper-clad bay, remaining open to natural light and the garden view without sacrificing comfort. The kitchen was relocated from the first floor to the garden level, with an adjacent formal dining room. Both rooms were enlarged from their previous iterations to accommodate weekly dinners with extended family. The kitchen includes a home office and breakfast nook, which doubles as a homework station. The cellar level was further excavated to accommodate finished storage space and a playroom where activity can be monitored from the kitchen workspaces.

CWB Architects

# BOERUM HILL GREEK REVIVAL

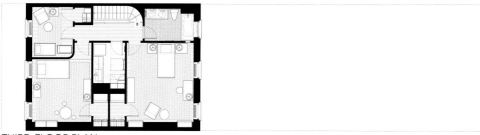

THIRD-FLOOR PLAN

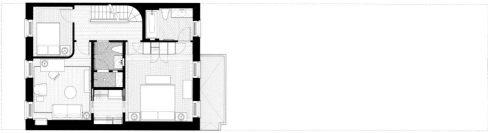

SECOND-FLOOR PLAN

FIRST-FLOOR PLAN

GROUND-FLOOR PLAN

0          12ft

The first floor is now reserved for entertaining. New pocket doors can be closed to separate the formal front parlor from the more relaxed back portion. At the end of the hall, a powder room with brass details, and a luxe bar, with antique-mirrored backsplash and stone tile flooring, leads to the deck and direct garden access. The width of the site allows for an ample interior program and extensive garden space, which includes a small lawn for play, an outdoor food preparation area, and rear zone for entertaining. The newly designed landscaping will continue to develop, further enhancing the yard's feeling of escape and filling in views from the kitchen and rear parlor above. A less visible but equally as conscious addition to the home is the rooftop PV solar array, which provides nearly 100 percent of the daily electrical usage, with the exception of the air-conditioning system on hot summer days.

Well-appointed interiors connect the home's traditional backdrop with a fresh take on classic design and functionality. Elegant but practical materials accommodate the family of five, and unique colors and patterns provide a luxurious atmosphere, while inviting residents and guests to relax and enjoy this classic Brooklyn brownstone.

Location **Brooklyn, New York** Area **4000 ft² (372 m²)** Completed **2015** Photography **Francis Dzikowski/OTTO**

The convenient location of this large lot in West Austin is what attracted the new owners, but the existing 1980s-era suburban brick house didn't align with their modern aesthetic, nor did it take advantage of the wooded natural setting.

A remodel and addition retained the core of the original structure and simplified the massing, removing extraneous gables and appendages. A light-filled living room and kitchen were added to the back of the house, opening to a new covered outdoor living space and negative-edge pool, with views into the woods. The added area improved the flow of the house, allowing it to serve both as a family house and space for frequent indoor/outdoor entertaining.

The front was reimagined with a modern volume containing a master bedroom and gym, connecting to the main house with a dramatic steel and glass dining room bridge. The entry was reconfigured to bring guests into the heart of the house, where a curved staircase retains the memory of the home's former design.

Furman + Keil Architects

# BRIDGE HOUSE

GROUND-FLOOR PLAN

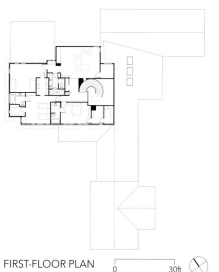

FIRST-FLOOR PLAN

0       30ft

Location **Austin, Texas** Area **6200 ft² (576 m²)** Completed **2016** Photography **Dror Baldinger**

The design brings a fresh material clarity to the house. Stucco on the exterior covers the old brick, retaining the thickness of the masonry, while providing a blank canvas for capturing shadows and light. Standing-seam metal roofing and siding bring a contemporary feel to the composition. The interior is simply defined with white walls, walnut casework, steel detailing, and slate and wood floors, giving new life to the house for a young family with three active boys.

This was the second historic Greek Revival project in a row from CWB Architects, and like the first, it required a complete structural rehabilitation. While the design aesthetic was approached with modern intentions, much of the original detailing was restored or reinterpreted to retain aspects of the original home's classic beauty.

The kitchen—the nucleus of the home—faces north, which would traditionally limit the amount of natural light received in the interior. To make the most of the available light, a floor-to-ceiling, steel-frame bay window was added, connecting to the uniquely appointed garden and adding just the right amount of floor space for a custom dining bench. In addition to the bench and custom-made kitchen stools, many of the furniture pieces are custom or recovered. All of the furnishings were selected and/or designed by the architects' own interior design team.

CWB Architects

# BROOKLYN HEIGHTS TAILORED MODERN

Location **Brooklyn Heights, New York**  Area **3100 ft² (288m²)**  Completed **2015**  Photography **Richard Powers**

THIRD-FLOOR PLAN

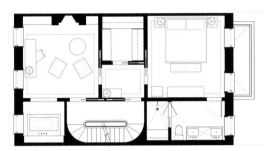

SECOND-FLOOR PLAN

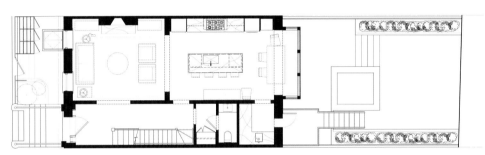

FIRST-FLOOR PLAN

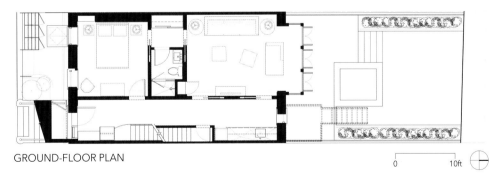

GROUND-FLOOR PLAN

0          10ft

This home is a deconstructed limestone cube with a rotated internal grid. The narrow three-story entry axial canyon brings natural light deep into the heart of the structure. Subtle level changes and carefully configured window openings gradually carve out space from the limestone cube, opening the home up toward the sky, eventually giving way to outdoor terraces shaded by cantilevered louvers, which further break down the overall massing.

The house is situated on a steep hillside above a dry creek. The formal genesis is threefold. Naturalistic, historic, and programmatic forces shape the house concurrently. In relation to its natural setting, it resembles large limestone boulders often chanced upon in the hill country by hikers; their natural beauty sculpted by gradual wind and water erosion over millions of years. Because Texas used to be under a pre-historic ocean, ancient coral reef and marine life forms, even dinosaur tracks, have been fossilized and encapsulated in time.

Bercy Chen Studio

# CARVED CUBE HOUSE

The marginalised notion that the DNA of a house can be captured in a single building block, establishing a relationship between the whole and the parts, was an idea the architects were interested in investigating. These ideas were overlaid with the logistical and programmatic requirement of the clients, as well as relationship to the geometry of the existing building below. Even though the sizable lot is close to an acre, the narrow shape and tight building setback lines imposed stringent restrictions on the building envelope.

Various stages of the design process were also inspired and informed by the architects' impression of stone quarry visits in the area. The home's spatial porosity pays homage to unique regional places such as the Longhorn Cavern. The project explores different textures of stone in a modern, three-dimensional re-interpretation of Renaissance concepts of rustication.

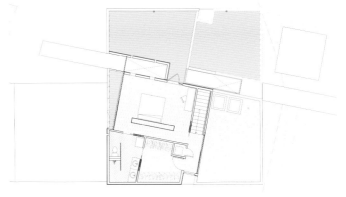

SECOND-FLOOR PLAN

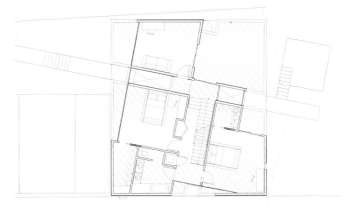

FIRST-FLOOR PLAN

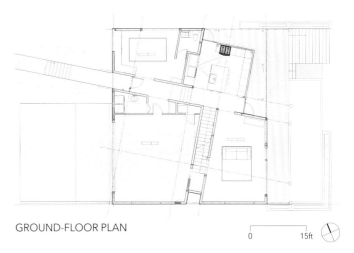

GROUND-FLOOR PLAN

0       15ft

Location **Fort Worth, Texas** Area **2900 ft² (269 m²)** Completed **2015** Photography **Paul Bardagjy Photography**

In a quaint San Francisco hillside neighborhood, this renovation and addition transformed a deteriorating Victorian house into a contemporary home filled with light and a rich palette of materials. In order to maintain the home's original scale and rhythm with neighboring homes, exterior improvements were primarily cosmetic, with new colors, moldings, and terraced gardens enhancing the façade.

The inside of the home was gutted and the roof reshaped, transforming it into a thoroughly modern environment. The entry leads into a spacious living, dining, kitchen, office, and powder room. High ceilings, skylights, and carefully placed windows create spaces shaped with light. Spectacular views of San Francisco from the living room balance intimate views to a sunny deck with glass railings and a colorful garden off the dining room, all reflected in a carefully placed mirror and glistening chandelier.

The home's interior, designed in close collaboration with the homeowner, Alessandra Taboni, includes bold touches of olive green, tangerine, sunflower yellow, and ruby red. Softly washed oak flooring, glass railings, white concrete counters and lacquered cabinets, stainless steel appliances, and floating fireplace give the interior a sense of drama.

House + House Architects

# CASA SAN FRANCISCO

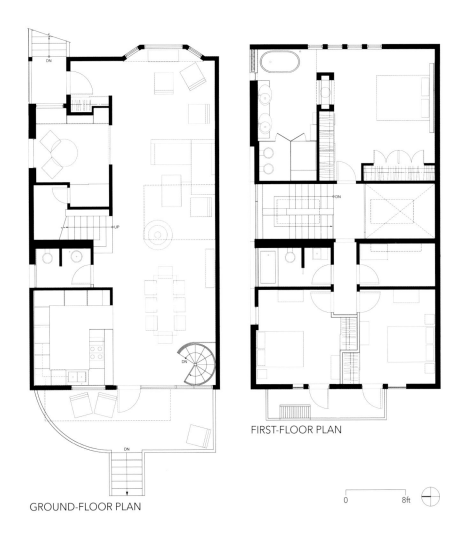

GROUND-FLOOR PLAN

FIRST-FLOOR PLAN

0          8ft

Gray concrete treads and red glass risers on the stairway to the first floor wrap around a custom glass wine cooler. Sculptural faucets and lights from Italy stand like art on the red powder room floor and hang throughout the home. Dramatic lighting, contemporary Italian furniture, and an eclectic collection of art and objects represent the owner's tastes, and meld comfortably with the refurbished spaces.

The newly shaped roof spans over three bedrooms and a double-height overlook from a bridge at the upper floor. A double-sided fireplace wrapped into a red glass closet links the master bedroom and bathroom. Carved stone sinks, a freestanding tub, and marble wrapped walls reflect in wide mirrors. Two children's bedrooms share a lively tiled bath and overlook the rear garden.

Location **San Francisco, California** Area **2100 ft² (210 m²)** Completed **2014** Photography **Steven and Cathi House**

This project is a remodel and addition to the last house designed by the internationally renowned architect and AIA Gold Medal winner, Charles W. Moore. The goal was clear: preserve the integrity and spirit of the original design, while adding to its utility and acknowledging the unique personality and preferences of the new owners.

The architects extended the existing entry porch by replicating the existing timber brackets and rotating them 90 degrees. A thin steel arbor sits atop these heavy beams, enhancing the depth and transition of the entry experience. New steel-and-glass doors further extend the entry connection to the interior. Additional glazing was incorporated into the existing dining room, providing more light, view, and access to the outdoors. The incorporation of new windows and doors into an existing armature of bookcases preserved the library-like quality of the space.

Furman + Keil Architects

# CIRCLE CANYON HOUSE

Location **Austin, Texas** Area **5513 ft² (512 m²)** Completed **2016** Photography **Paul Bardagjy Photography**

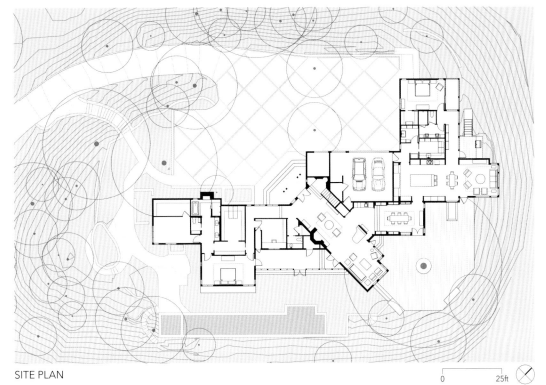

SITE PLAN

0     25ft

A new family room was added to the kitchen wing of the house, along with a patterned wood ceiling taking cues from the existing living room woodwork and providing a counterbalance to the kitchen's soaring volume. A new outdoor deck incorporates the hilltop view and provides outdoor circulation between the dining, kitchen, and family room. The guest wing was completely reconfigured and repurposed. An existing narrow porch was converted to an interior circulation space, allowing access to a new guest bedroom and bathroom. In the master bathroom, existing skylight shafts were reshaped and expanded, providing more daylight, while bringing new stone and tile finishes into focus.

The late Charles Moore wrote that a home is not complete until the occupants claim the space and make it their own, inhabiting rooms with their own personalities, furnishings, and ideas. It is the architects' belief that he would embrace the changes to his work, knowing that the act of habitation continues and the owners call the place home.

Located in one of Seattle's densest and most established residential areas, City Cabin's design realizes the client's vision for a private urban retreat that would connect them to nature. The house sits on the northwest corner of the lot, maximizing garden areas on the south and east sides. Its staggered footprint allows for more glazing, increasing sun exposure and garden views. The home's net-zero design incorporates key sustainability features, while the integration of trees and dense greenery onto the site transforms an ordinary urban infill lot into a private refuge.

The home is organized into two wings, with the bedrooms, storage, laundry, and pantry areas extending in opposite directions off the home's central gathering space. This central area is a single volume defined by a 16-foot-high (5-meter-high) ceiling. A full-height window wall in the main living area overlooks the gardens to the southeast, creating a visual connection to the outdoors, while clerestory windows maximize solar gains and create a sense of lightness while maintaining privacy.

Olson Kundig

# CITY CABIN

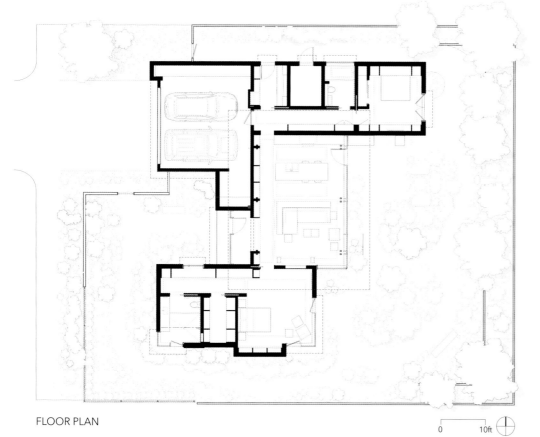

FLOOR PLAN

0        10ft

Materials and assemblies were chosen primarily for economy and sustainability, but the palette also draws inspiration from the client's extensive Native American art collection. The concrete floors are tinted with a custom red hue, while walls and ceilings are made from A/C grade plywood, chosen for its durability and simplicity. On the exterior, fir siding reclaimed from a nearby fruit storage warehouse will weather naturally with minimal maintenance. Durable galvanized steel roofing and beam end caps complement the natural wood finishes, developing a rich patina with exposure. Along with reclaimed materials, the house incorporates several green strategies such as a green roof, photovoltaic panels, and an air-to-water heat pump, reflecting the client's longstanding engagement with environmental conservation.

Location **Seattle, Washington** Area **2400 ft² (223 m²)** Completed **2015** Photography **Aaron Leitz**

This loft-like modern treehouse has been assembled with an inverted floorplan, positioning the primary living spaces on the top floor for maximum light exposure. This opens up views of the famous Hollywood sign, fitting for the screenwriting owner. The home's design is motivated by mid-century style, but also expresses a sense of California-cool. The second story sits slightly pulled back on all sides to make room for peripheral skylights, allowing natural light to permeate into the lower levels.

Upon entry, one is greeted by an impressive three-story atrium, accented by steel-framed glass floors and topped with pitched-roof ceilings. Glass is a prominent material used throughout the residence, seen from the very top of the structure in the form of expansive skylights and layered all the way down through the various stories of walkways, allowing natural light to stream through all levels of the home. A living tree is stationed on the ground level, sprouting up through the multi-tier stairwell.

Abramson Teiger Architects

# COHEN RESIDENCE

The top level of the home holds a family room, living room, eat-in kitchen, and dining area. These spaces expand upon one another for accessibility and a sense of community. Private bedrooms are situated on the ground floor. At the basement level there is an office/screening room and art studio. Natural materials, such as warm wood paneling and neutral-toned CMU, are accented by pops of color in the interior design choices. Family-friendly furniture was mostly custom made and complements the vibrant art collection.

BASEMENT FLOOR PLAN

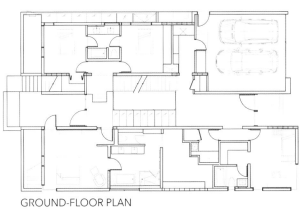

GROUND-FLOOR PLAN

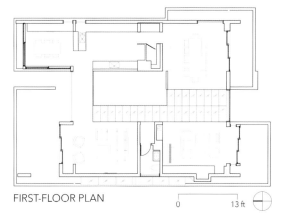

FIRST-FLOOR PLAN

0       13 ft

Location **Los Angeles, California** Area **6000 ft² (557 m²)** Completed **2013** Photography **Jim Bartsch**

This new home is part of an enclave of eight houses built in suburban Chicago by well-known North Shore developer Charles Hemphill. Known as Milburn Park and built between 1937 and 1939, the houses were designed by Hemphill's architect Raymond Houlihan. They all featured lannon-stone exteriors, with cut stone classical entryways and dark-stained entry doors. After the war a ranch-style house and a small red brick colonial were built on two of the four lots fronting Lake Michigan. The colonial was torn down as the site for this house.

The new house has a formal lannon-stone front, garage, cut-stone classical entryway, and dark-stained wood front door. The back of the house is treated as an interlocking volume sided in painted wood boards, with a large screen porch and first-floor balcony as a more informal and picturesque response to the lake. The ground floor has been designed as an open plan, with classical columns, beamed ceilings, and wide-cased openings with interior transom windows defining spaces. The interior living spaces, bedrooms, and master bathroom all enjoy views of the lake. All of the home's furnishings were chosen by JamesThomas Interiors.

Cohen & Hacker Architects

# CONTEXTUAL HOUSE

Designed to accommodate the special needs and limited mobility of two of the family's children, this home is intended to serve them through adulthood. The design seeks to enrich the girls' lives by creating a variety of spatial experiences animated by the constant movement of natural light.

The linear plan alternates clusters of living spaces with three courtyards, arranging them along a 125-foot (38-meter) circulation spine. The generous perimeter offers every major space direct access to the exterior, while a series of roof monitors bring additional light in from above. Daylight enters every space year round from dawn to dusk, creating an ever-changing play of shadow and reflection, while views to the exterior provide interest as changing seasons and weather interact with carefully designed landscapes.

The home's exterior spaces also offer a variety of sensory experiences. A low concrete wall radiates warmth to the adjacent sitting area, a fountain with shallow basins allows soaking of hands and feet, a courtyard offers a small lawn and flowering tree, and a patio with an outdoor fireplace gives way to rolling grass-covered berms.

Kuklinski + Rappe Architects

# COURTYARD RESIDENCE

The home addresses the girls' health and well-being. Indirect lighting is used throughout to minimize glare when the girls are reclined, in-slab geothermal radiant heating ensures their comfort when engaged in activities on the floor, materials were selected to minimize off-gassing, whole-house fans supplement operable windows to provide fresh air, and energy-recovery ventilators ensure indoor air quality during cold weather.

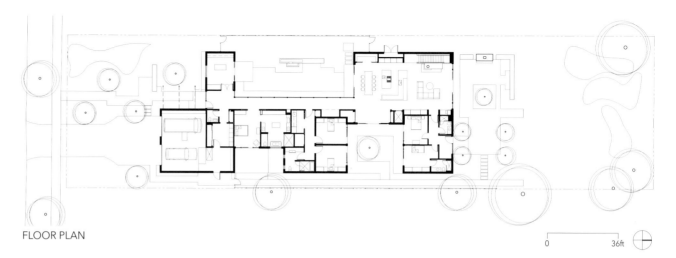

FLOOR PLAN

0                36ft

Location **DuPage County, Illinois** Area **4900 ft² (455 m²)** Completed **2016**
Landscaping: **Barker Evans Landscape Architecture** Photography **Tom Harris Photography**

Located on a narrow site facing the Deschutes River, this project was sited to preserve a beautiful stone ledge close to the water. All major spaces within the home open up to the river, with a main wood deck hovering a few inches above the stone.

The main living space has large, 8-by-8-foot (2.5-by-2.5-meter) sliding glass panels opening to both the river and south-facing courtyard on the opposite side. The courtyard provides a quiet and contemplative space, in contrast to the busy and active river side of the house. Upstairs, the master bathroom cantilevers dramatically out toward the river, allowing a freestanding tub to visually float over the river traffic. The master bedroom and study also enjoy spectacular river views.

The home's exterior is clad with two different types of siding: tightly spaced Western red cedar and corrugated metal siding. The cedar is stained a natural wood color, contrasting with the zinc gray color of the metal siding. The roofing material is a standing seam metal, also in zinc gray. The warm tones of the wood are juxtaposed against the cool tones of the metal siding and roofing. The fireplace chimney is clad in Montana ledge stone with a combination of earth tones and gray-blue colors. The house was designed to be a sustainable structure from the start, with 40 percent higher insulation values than required by code.

FINNE Architects

# DESCHUTES HOUSE

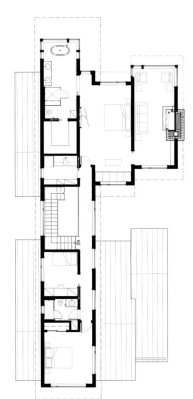

FIRST-FLOOR PLAN

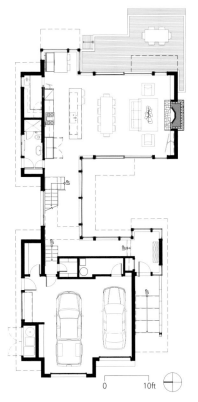

GROUND-FLOOR PLAN

0          10ft

In the main interior space, two curvilinear wood ceiling panels are suspended over the living and dining areas. Each panel has 60 uniquely shaped wood slats, tightly spaced in order to create an abstracted river landscape. Other notable interior details include: a folded steel fireplace mantle, the suspended glass kitchen island cabinet (with LED lighting), and a sculptural steel, glass, and wood staircase. These details are a reflection of a modern home enhanced by beautifully crafted materials and surfaces—crafted modernism.

Location **Oregon** Area **2950 ft² (274 m²)** Completed **2015** Photography **Benjamin Benschneider**

Located on a triangular site abutting a mountain, Doheny boasts incredible views of Los Angeles below. By manipulating the site, which at first seemed almost unbuildable, the architects were able to achieve an 8000-square-foot (743-square-meter) home. The client's desire to maximize views and create a significant entry were the project's greatest challenges.

As a starting point, the architects used retaining walls to cut back the topography to provide a building pad. This created a unique curving wall that followed the contours of the mountain, making it the perfect space for a water feature. The home's entry sequence follows the water wall, which draws the eye to the spectacular view when crossing a bridge to the entry door. A basement courtyard design with water spilling from above into a basin below, traversed by bridges on both levels, solved the need for light in the lower level. The water feature bounces light into the rooms below. With entertaining in mind, the lower-level living space is finished with a full bar, gaming lounge, media room, and gym.

McClean Design

# DOHENY

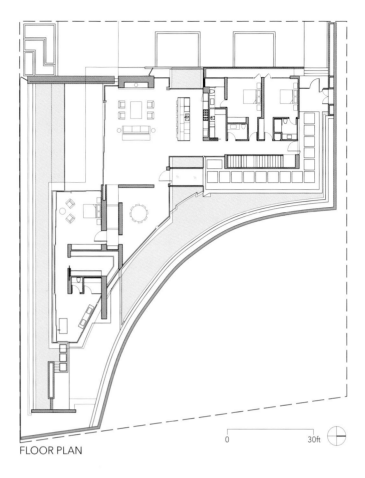

FLOOR PLAN

0              30ft

The living room and outdoor patio are seamlessly connected, with an infinity-edge pool running the entire length of the view. The kitchen enjoys views of the home's entry and water feature, while wall-to-wall skylights flood the space with light.

The dining room is framed by a water wall and impressive wine display. A compact master bedroom opens completely to the pool and view, and the bathroom enjoys a quiet outdoor garden with fireplace and patio.

Dove Cottage, commissioned by clients for whom the architect had previously designed a maisonette in a new building on Chicago's Gold Coast, was conceived as an ancillary residence to their existing, somewhat larger main weekend residence. It is a place for guests—particularly children and grandchildren—and venue for summer musicales, as well as a more manageable home tailored to future needs.

Designed to give the appearance of a true cottage, its modest appearance belies its spacious and varied interiors. Angled wings extend from the broad, shingled gable roof over the central mass, and a continuous porch facing Lake Michigan unifies the composition.

At the center of the plan, the great room, like the center hall of a shingle-style house, has been articulated into areas for dining, reading, relaxing by the fireplace, or watching television. The room is specifically designed for music performances, with space around the grand concert piano for 60 guests.

Robert A. M. Stern Architects, Randy Correll, Partner

# DOVE COTTAGE

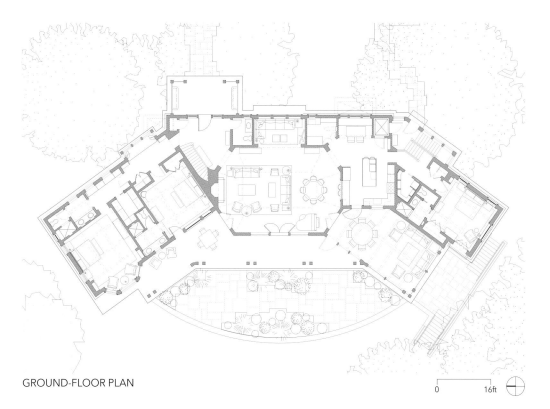

GROUND-FLOOR PLAN

0    16ft

The home's great room—an extended octagon in plan—opens to covered porches and connects to the entry hall, kitchen, and breakfast room. Bedrooms are housed in angled wings on the first floor. The lower level accommodates a day-lit playroom, movie room, and an octagonal room decorated with a whimsical pictorial map of the Great Lakes and beyond. All interior design was completed by Arthur Dunnam for Jed Johnson Studio.

Location **Lakeside, Michigan** Area **9700 ft² (900 m²)** Completed **2016** Photography **Peter Aaron/OTTO**

Situated on the west side of Lake George, the house has been designed as a retreat for a young family. The clients envisioned a home that would essentially utilize the same footprint as the seasonal one-story camp that has occupied the property since the 1950s, while incorporating their admiration for Japanese architecture and simple open plans.

In response, the design team created a blended home, which combines western and northeastern architectural influences. An open living area, kitchen, dining arrangement, and master bedroom suite occupy the ground-floor program. A guest room, media room and office occupy the lower-level walk out. Children's bedrooms and bathroom are located on the first floor in the upper level of the pagoda inspired geometry.

Knowing that the home would be used mostly on weekends, with the possibility of visitors, the plan utilized a large screened porch and deck, allowing the main living space to expand and open through a series of 8-foot-high (2.5-meter-high) sliding glass doors. When open, the functional floor plan expands by more than 50 percent, providing highly sought-after summer sleeping spaces.

Phinney Design Group

# EAST MEETS WEST IN THE ADIRONDACKS

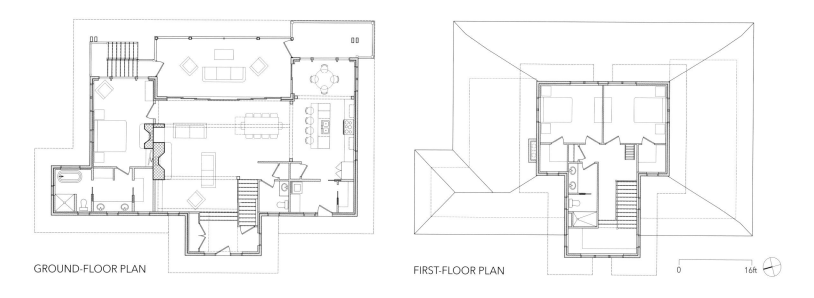

GROUND-FLOOR PLAN

FIRST-FLOOR PLAN

0        16ft

The home pursues a silver LEED certification. A geothermal heating and cooling system, combined with a high-performance thermal envelope and LED lighting, greatly decreases energy use. Structural Insulated Panels (SIPs) and radiant barriers have been used for the roof, allowing for a series of vaulted spaces in the kitchen, master bedroom, and upstairs bedrooms while maintaining a well-insulated exterior envelope.

Local and regional materials have been incorporated into the home. Rustic white oak flooring and stairs, live edge walnut accents, and built-ins composed of white oak painted poplar were all made and installed by a local carpenter. Reclaimed barn beams and barn-siding wainscoting add a rustic contrast to the white and gray color scheme. Exterior siding is a combination of locally milled Douglas fir timbers, eastern white bark on cedar planks, poplar bark shakes and New Baltimore stone, which was quarried close to the project site.

The home has been designed as a sustainable retreat to accommodate the family as it grows, with the clients hoping to retire at the property later in life.

Location **Hague, New York** Area **3829 ft² (356 m²)** Completed **2016** Photography **Elizabeth Pedinotti Haynes**

Located in Seattle, on a narrow site facing Puget Sound, this home's architectural massing wraps around a south-facing courtyard containing a large reflecting pool with two floating basalt boulders. The reflecting pool gathers all roof drainage from the house, with the downspout from the living room roof providing a 10-foot (three-meter) waterfall. The main living space has sweeping westerly views of Puget Sound and the Olympic Mountains, contrasting with the intimacy and serenity created by the courtyard and reflecting pool on the east side.

A strong sense of crafted modernism is present in the home. Exposed wood beams in the living space change pitch along the length of the room, providing a sense of drama as the roof unfolds toward landscape views. Upstairs, tall glass walls wrap the master bedroom on three sides, providing stunning panoramic views as it cantilevers out toward the water and mountains.

A waterjet-cut steel fence and gate lead to the home's entry. Stainless-steel stands elevate the basalt boulders in the reflecting pool, allowing them to hover slightly above the water's surface.

FINNE Architects

# ELLIOTT BAY HOUSE

GROUND-FLOOR PLAN

FIRST-FLOOR PLAN

0          20ft

Exterior siding is custom-stained red cedar, with two different patterns and colors. The striking steel-and-wood stairs have waterjet-cut steel railings, with a pattern based on hand-drawn ink brush strokes. The rusted steel entry gate uses the same ink brush pattern, only reversed. The beech interior cabinets have a custom topographic CNC-milled pattern, and freeform steel-lighting bars in the ceiling tie the kitchen and dining spaces together.

Highly energy efficient and sustainable, the home is insulated 40 percent higher than the required code. All roof drainage is directed to the reflecting pool for collection and a radiant, hydronic heat system allows lower operating temperatures and higher occupant comfort levels. Gypcrete has been used for radiant tubes, which conserve heat and provide great warmth and comfort for the feet. Generous glass areas provide natural lighting and ventilation, while large overhangs have been used for sun and rain protection. All interior wood is FSC certified; LED lighting and water-conserving plumbing fixtures have been used throughout the house; and windows have built-in shading. The house has been pre-wired for photovoltaic roof panels, and an electric vehicle charging station has been installed in the garage.

Location **Seattle, Washington** Area **3425 ft² (318 m²)** Completed **2015** Photography **Benjamin Benschneider**

Designed by two architects for their retirement, this compound is sited on a bluff overlooking the Connecticut River, and comprises an extensive list of features including: a guesthouse, greenhouse, orchard, ballet studio, woodworking shop, root cellar, and secret passage within the main house.

After tearing down the existing house, the new project was built in seven steps. The owners, an architect and former professional ballerina turned architect, wanted to feel fully integrated with nature. The home's earthy colors, stone exteriors, zinc roofing, and curving shapes are at harmony with the natural surrounds. Even the windows have fanciful plant-shaped muntins and the stone walls curve in an alliance with the river. The home is heated and cooled by a geothermal system. It is well insulated and does not require direct use of fossil fuels.

Both the guesthouse and main house command panoramic views of the river. The whole complex, including the two barns, assumes a low, horizontal profile of gently sloping roofs, which merge with the site and recall rolling hills in the distance.

Centerbrook Architects

# THE eMBARKERDARO

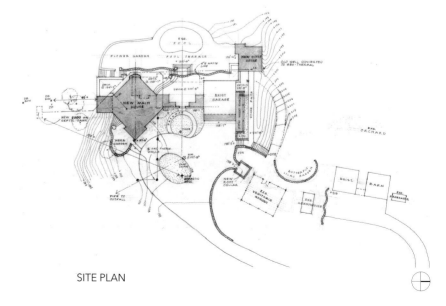

SITE PLAN

The house can be lived in, on, and all around, expressing a freedom of movement. Handmade dancing flowers frame display niches, while berries adorn the bay windows, and a graceful swan neck provides a newel post. A sculpture of a sentinel mountain lion, made by a friend, gazes out to the horizon. Surrounding the dance studio, a painted frieze depicts the owners' favourite illustrators.

Not only is this project a magnificent home, it is also an example of an intricate and memorable living experience that engages all of the senses.

Location **Lower Connecticut River Valley, Connecticut** Area **13,700 ft² (1273 m²)** Completed **2017** Photography **Nathaniel Riley**

131

Owned by Davis Factor, this project began as a series of site improvements around an existing single-story, mid-century home. A new carport, swimming pool, IPE wood deck, and cabana in the rear yard, with views of the San Fernando Valley below, were added to the home.

Because the original post-and-beam structure took advantage of valley views through frameless glass it was preserved upon construction. The new carport and cabana were designed with exposed-steel, structural members.

Factor seized the opportunity to purchase the lot next door, more than doubling the size of his property and setting the design tone for an estate-type setting. This increase in land size allowed for the construction of a guesthouse. An exposed concrete wall bisects the guesthouse, acting as a datum between public and private spaces, with a spacious living room/bar on one side, and master suite on the other. The driveway— an elongated entry experience—is a combination of concrete pavers and permeable grasscrete.

Christopher Mercier, (fer) studio

# FACTOR RESIDENCE

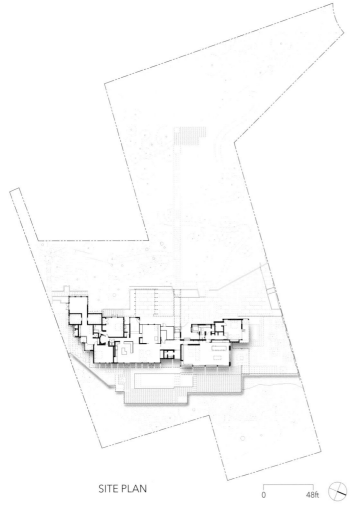

SITE PLAN

0       48ft

Location **Los Angeles, California** Area **6700 ft² (622 m²)** Completed **2014** Photography **Josh White**

Sarah Buxton Design completed the interiors for the original portion of the home and worked with (fer) studio for the addition. The spaces were inspired by the client's love of black-and-white photography. The entrance was intended to feel like a gallery—a place to sit and relax, while enjoying spectacular views and artwork. A blend of modern and mid-century pieces, such as hand-woven rugs and collectable art, emit a sense of timeless appeal throughout the home.

In terms of sustainability, the project was organized and designed to preserve existing drainage patterns. Catch basins tied to new subsurface storm drain lines provide an effective means of water collection, while the general and relatively unchanged permeability of the site allows for continued natural recapture. Most of the home's materials were sourced or fabricated locally and include: wood, steel, concrete, stucco, drywall, sheet metal, and millwork.

This three-bedroom home on Big Sur's spectacular south coast, is anchored in the natural beauty and power of the Californian landscape. The design strategy behind the home was to embed the building into the land to create a structure inseparable from its context. Despite offering dramatic views—a 250-foot drop to the Pacific Ocean along the bluff and western exposure—the site demanded a form more complex than a giant picture window.

The long, thin volume conforms and deforms to the natural contours of the land and the geometries of the bluff. In this way, the complex structural system applies and defies natural forms to accommodate the site. The house is cantilevered 12-feet (4-meters) back from the bluff, both to protect the cliff's delicate ecosystem and to ensure the structure's integrity and safety. The interior is a shelter; a refuge in contrast with the roughness and immense scale of the ocean and cliff. The house also shields the southern outdoor spaces from the powerful winds that blow from the northwest.

Fougeron Architecture

# FALL HOUSE

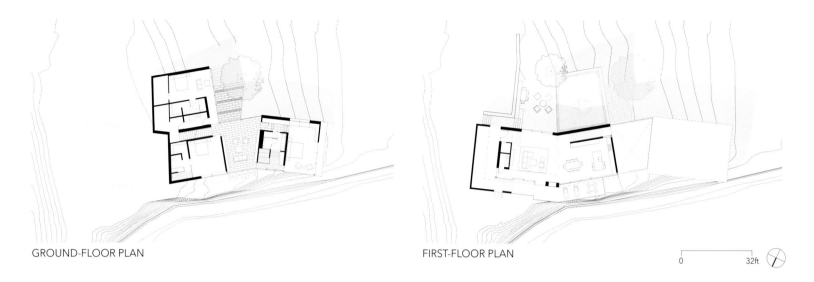

GROUND-FLOOR PLAN

FIRST-FLOOR PLAN

0     32ft

Location **Big Sur, California** Area **3800 ft² (353 m²)** Completed **2014** Photography **Joe Fletcher**

The main body of the house is composed of two rectangular boxes connected by an all-glass library/den. The main entry is located at the top of the upper volume, with the living spaces unfolding from the most public to the most private. The living room, kitchen, and dining room are an open plan with subtle changes in levels and roof planes to differentiate various functions. The lower volume, a double-cantilevered master-bedroom suite, acts as a promontory above the ocean, offering breathtaking views from its floor-to-ceiling windows. The link between these two volumes is the glass library/den; it is the hearth of the structure, a room that unites the house inside and out, both with its geometry and its transparency. A one-story concrete wing, perpendicular to the house, locks the structure to the land and includes a ground-floor bedroom, building services, and a green roof.

The house has two main façades. The south one is clad in copper, which wraps up the wall and over onto the roof. Copper-clad roof overhangs protect windows and the front door from the sun and ocean winds. The façade to the north is made of all glass, opening the home to the view.

Located on a two-acre waterfront lot in North Haven, this home was designed to take advantage of the views across Sag Harbor to the southeast, while drawing late afternoon through the home and into multiple outdoor entertaining spaces for as long as possible.

Entry to the home is gained by passing under a first-floor bedroom wing or 'ceremonial threshold' into an open-air courtyard. Here, views of the patio spaces, pool, and harbour are revealed through wall-to-wall glass panels that open on both sides, accommodating an entertaining space and true indoor/outdoor lifestyle.

A roof deck and outdoor fireplace over the one-story wing allow for late-day/early-evening sunsets without interrupting views from any first-floor spaces.

This seven-bedroom, eight-bathroom home also includes two powder rooms, an office, family room, and multiple outdoor spaces. It is clad in a combination of limestone panels, teak, and glass.

Blaze Makoid Architecture

# FERRY ROAD

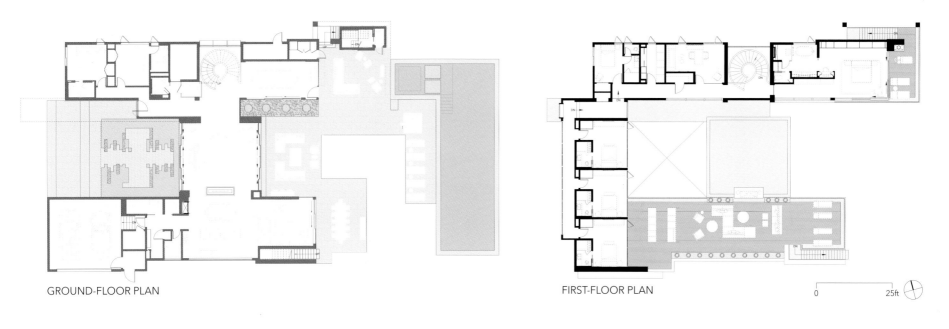

GROUND-FLOOR PLAN

FIRST-FLOOR PLAN

0                    25ft

Location **North Haven, New York** Area **7500 ft² (697 m²)** Completed **2015** Photography **Joshua McHugh**

Fogland Point on Rhode Island's Sakonnet River is known for its ever-changing weather and harsh winds. The site, although a private, west-facing field with great views of the river, is prone to extreme weather.

The area's microclimate aggravated the goals of the energy conscious owners who wanted an eco-friendly, minimal-upkeep house, with a strong connection to the outdoors. They also felt strongly about having a home that was low profile, minimizing visual impact from the water. The program, as a result, was for a main living/dining/kitchen area, three-bedrooms, den, office, porch, and separate boat house/garage, with living space above for guests.

Similar to the many multiple-building farms in the region, the program was broken down into parts, with the massing used to create sheltered outdoor spaces. A two-story bedroom wing was set to the north to block winter winds and to form protected terraces to the east and west of the central living area. The narrow building profiles, window placement, and sliding louvered shutters, promote cross ventilation and minimize summer heat gain.

Estes Twombly Architects

# FOGLAND HOUSE

FIRST-FLOOR PLAN

GROUND-FLOOR PLAN

0        20ft

With the use of deep overhangs, porches, terraces, and stone walls, the owners can enjoy the outdoors with various degrees of shelter throughout the day and seasons. Triple-glazed windows, double wall/roof insulation, and high efficiency mechanical and fresh air systems help keep energy costs down. The house is also prewired for a seven-kilowatt solar array on the boathouse roof. Durable metal roofing, slate siding, and stone terraces were used on the exterior. In the interior, tiled floors have been used for the primary ground-floor circulation areas, and eastern white oak flooring and cabinets have been used elsewhere.

**Location** Tiverton, Rhode Island **Area** 4200 ft² (390 m²) **Completed** 2014 **Photography** Warren Jagger

Perched atop a tree-covered knoll on a 320-acre (129-hectare) site in West Paso Robles, California, this magnificent home was designed around three multi-trunked oak trees. The structure becomes one with the site as it weaves around the trees, integrating with nature and framing views in all directions.

The design process began with an initial program created by the architect and client. From there, a floor plan was devised, delineated, and set into a mock-up site, followed by the creation of a study model for the structure, which took five months to complete. Each space was then studied relative to scale in order to understand what the space might feel like. After several months examining the model, the architect met with the client to review and approve the completed model. When approved, the structure was scaled from the model and working drawings were created for the commencement of construction.

Materials used include steel, wood, glass, and smooth Portland cement plaster. The straightforward post-and-beam structure utilizes steel I-beams and steel tube columns, with jaw-dropping cantilevered overhangs, 25 feet (8 meters) to 50 feet (15 meters), and steel I-beams spanning up to 100 feet (30 meters), as impressive and distinctive features of the home.

Norm Applebaum Architect

# FOX HOLLOW

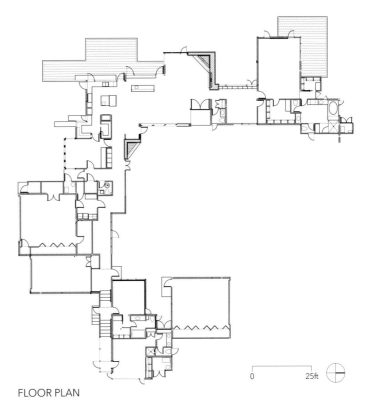

FLOOR PLAN

0          25ft

Location **Paso Robles, California** Area **4357 ft² (405 m²)** Completed **2015** Photography **John Durant**

Built on a historic landmark lot, the original 1890s home was picked up and placed on a new foundation to make way for the project. The home's design required approval from Aspen's Historic Preservation Commission and needed to stand on its own while remaining contextual to its historical surrounds.

Inspired by the residential vernacular of Aspen's historic West End neighborhood, this home brings a sense of clarity and elegance to a traditionally ornate Victorian form. With the clients' personal and professional lifestyle in mind, the design intends to accommodate a large number of guests for entertaining, while also providing a sense of intimacy for private relaxation. The open plan connects indoor and outdoor spaces with seamless lift-and-slide pocket doors. Interiors feature custom built-ins, floating furnishings, and custom fixtures.

Pure in form and modern articulation, the home is contemporary and efficient with no space unused. A simple gable roof, patterned siding, and traditional front porch are an ode to Aspen's Victorian past. A small bridge over a stream in the front entry path accents the minimal landscaping, while the purity and execution of detailing further distinguish the home's identity, bringing greater clarity to the traditional gable form.

Rowland+Broughton

# GAME ON

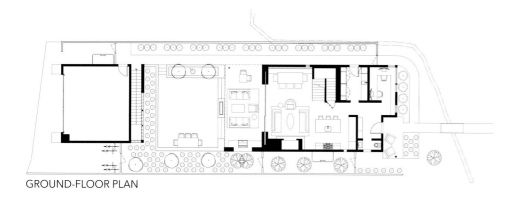

GROUND-FLOOR PLAN

FIRST-FLOOR PLAN

0          20ft

Location **Aspen, Colorado** Area **4291 ft² (399 m²)** Completed **2015** Photography **Brent Hoss Photography**

Located in Redondo Beach, this house has simple massing accentuated by articulated openings situated and designed to frame views of the ocean and the surrounding mountains. The geometry used to create the system of apertures continues throughout the interior. Pattern and openings differentiate interior surfaces that define zones of circulation and the major living spaces. The spaces are layered with the use of pattern and light to create an experiential architecture.

The home consists of three stories and has been designed with an open floor plan. The living spaces open to several private outdoor terraces, including a roof-top garden, which takes advantage of the surrounding views. The home is environmentally sound, with sustainable strategies including photovoltaics for power and a solar hydronic system for the heating of water. The latest in green technologies, materials, and building systems have been used throughout. The distinct form of the building optimizes airflow, natural light, and sun protection.

Patrick Tighe Architecture

# GARRISON RESIDENCE

BASEMENT PLAN

GROUND-FLOOR PLAN     FIRST-FLOOR PLAN     SECOND-FLOOR PLAN     ROOF PLAN

0     20ft

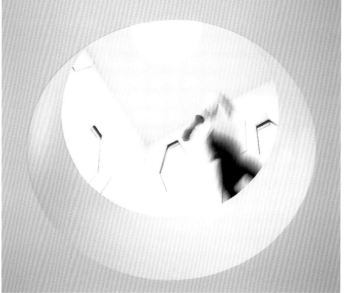

Location **Los Angeles, California** Area **3500 ft² (325 m²)** Completed **2015** Photography **Art Gray**

Created for everyday living, intimate meetings, and occasional entertaining, this home was intended to foster a sense of community. Architecturally, the project was designed to capture views, bring in daylight, and establish a sense of calm through simplicity and open space.

Due to the views, which impressively progress as one moves up through the house, the main living space is on the top floor. This space opens up at both ends with views of the city from the living room at one end and the kitchen and terraced yard at the other end. Other notable design elements include a floating fireplace wall, polished stainless-steel ceiling above the dining table, and steel/glass/wood staircase, which drops down through all floors and acts as a vertical counterpoint. Overall, the space encompasses a white minimalism, balanced with wood, color, and the city beyond.

The study, music room, and master suite are one level down. The master bathroom's floors and walls are made of carefully selected and matched Carrara marble slabs, which contrast with dark fixtures to evoke a spa-like atmosphere. The ground floor has a guest suite and media lounge. The house has a two-story entry with a red pivot door. Wide-plank, reclaimed Douglas fir features in most rooms and has been used for the staircase in combination with blackened steel and glass.

The home's charcoal exterior is a result of *shou sugi ban* (traditional Japanese charred wood). This technique renders the material less flammable and also gives the home a distinct identity.

CCS Architecture

# GLEN PARK RESIDENCE

With a gallery-worthy view of the Santa Monica Bay, Glenhaven Residence was designed to showcase the majesty of the outside world. Bright white interior spaces are punctuated with dark exterior materials to mimic a framed work of art: where the bustling city meets the Pacific Ocean as the subject. The owners were ready for a downsized home that would reflect the more mature pace of their current lifestyle. No longer in need of massive spaces and countless rooms, the couple bought a classic and relatively small ranch-style house with a glamorous view of Los Angeles.

The existing structure was stripped down to the studs so it could be rebuilt with crisp lines and modern figurations. From the front entrance to the back patio, the structure acts as a portal that celebrates views of the striking scenery from every room.

Abramson Teiger Architects

# GLENHAVEN RESIDENCE

Inside, an open and fluid layout makes the smaller space feel more voluminous, finished with minimal and cool-toned neutrals. In addition to the master suite, guest bedroom, living room, kitchen, and dining area, a home office for two is situated at the main entrance.

The back of the home opens up both visually and physically to create an indoor/outdoor environment where the owners can enjoy the Southern California weather. Interior space and materials extend onto the patio under a cantilevered overhang, which shelters an outdoor living area. To maintain unobstructed views, the patio has been left without railings. Instead, a low-profile fire pit acts as a safety guard. Exterior materials were selected for their desired low maintenance. Trespa, Swiss Pearl, and metal siding wrap the façade and create a refined, simple, and modern look.

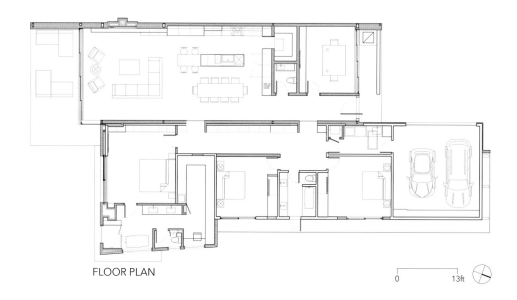

FLOOR PLAN

0    13ft

Location **Pacific Palisades, California** Area **3000 ft² (278 m²)** Completed **2014** Photography **Jim Bartsch**

Seated on a heavily wooded bluff, this home tempers views of the expansive Nueces River Valley to the southwest and a bowl-shaped ridge encircling the site's northern half. A wood-crafted arbor covered in vines welcomes guests through an entry breezeway, with shade, dramatic dapplings of light, and direct views to Goat Mountain.

The breezeway unites the home's two volumes: a main living area to the west, and a master suite and library to the east. Open and spacious, the main living area connects the living room, kitchen, and dining in one volume. A reading nook adjoins the living room as a cozy place to watch wildlife.

East of the breezeway, a simple stone parapet box houses the library/guest room and laundry/storage space. Another shed roof floats over the stone parapet to form the master bedroom, with great views made private by the stone parapet box.

Lake|Flato Architects

# GOAT MOUNTAIN RANCH

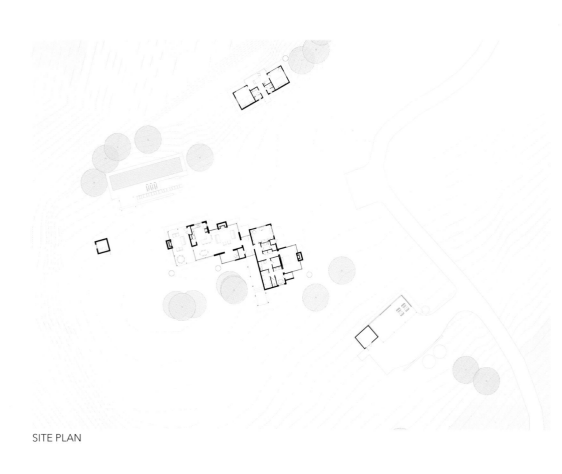

SITE PLAN

Location **Uvalde, Texas** Area indoor: **4120 ft² (383 m²)** outdoor: **2412 ft² (224 m²)** Completed **2015** Photography **Casey Dunn, Ryann Ford**

The home is outfitted in gracefully weathering, natural and local materials, with some collected by the owner over time from their family's Louisiana farm. Reclaimed-wood siding has been incorporated in ceilings and interior walls, while steel kettles, once used for boiling sugar, have been reinterpreted as water catchment containers for the rainwater system. These reclaimed materials provide Goat Mountain Ranch with both a rich patina and reverent nod to the owner's family history.

173

The client wanted a manageable second home with a boat dock to accommodate extended family and friends, as well as a love of fishing. Located on a seven-acre (three-hectare) site, with a wetlands buffer to the water, this Hamptons site was an ideal spot to moor a boat with easy access to the ocean.

A series of simple rectangular boxes form the structure of this contemporary home. Contrasting materials—durable white Azek and dark weathered oak, thermally modified to withstand harsh weather conditions—dramatically offset the box design. Large glass windows and doors allow for ocean views on the first floor, while light and expansive views of the bay are enjoyed throughout the rest of the home. Interior wall surfaces of weathered oak and white enhance the home's simple material palate, creating a sense of continuity. The home features an open plan for public spaces, plus five bedrooms and six baths, ideal for relaxed summer use and entertaining.

Austin Patterson Disston Architects

# HAMPTONS MODERN ON THE BAY

Double-height windows afford the open staircase views of the ocean. A functional boot room, accessed from a secondary front entry, allows for direct communication to the rear yard amenities, and is a good access point from the beach and boating activities. Use of sliding-wall components and pocket doors throughout the home allow for flexibility in the overall living experience.

A pool and an additional 3655-square-foot (340-square-meter) deck on the upper and ground floors provides space for outdoor enjoyment. Allocating an almost equal amount of space to outdoor and indoor areas is a balance not often achieved, and is what makes this project both an intimate family home and, due to ample room, the ideal space for a gathering.

Location **Hamptons, New York** Area **4500 ft² (418 m²)** Completed **2016** Photography **Tria Giovan**

GROUND-FLOOR PLAN

FIRST-FLOOR PLAN

0　　　　　16ft

A desire to clearly express the beauty of simple honest construction and basic materials characterizes this renovation of a 1950s ranch house in a lakeside Michigan community. The property has been in the possession of the owner since 1974 and although its roof was caving in and its slab was slowly sinking, the size and general layout of the house were effective. These factors led to the decision to renovate rather than demolish the house.

Two new load-bearing lines were added in the middle of the structure in the form of steel-pipe columns. What appear to be continuous gable trusses, spanning the full width of the house, are in fact two sets of independent shed trusses linked via pin connections to the catwalk along the new column lines. The kitchen was repositioned to a more central position and exposed wood trusses, polished concrete floors, zinc-coated walls and roofing, galvanized metal grating, and white stucco are offset by crimson-red casement windows, reflecting a more contemporary lifestyle. A screened porch—the epicenter of the home—distinguishes the street-side façade and provides a direct connection to the surrounding gardens.

Searl Lamaster Howe Architects

# HARBERT COTTAGE

FLOOR PLAN

0       15ft

Passive measures have been used wherever possible to conserve energy, and large overhangs and reflective roof materials greatly reduce cooling requirements. Structural Insulated Panels (SIPs) form the roofs, expediting the construction process and providing exceptionally high insulation value. A geothermal well feeds a radiant heating system embedded in the floor. The heat pump also pre-warms water for domestic hot water needs. The heat load of the porch is relieved by its open clerestory, which naturally pulls hot air up and out of the structure. Local sourcing was used wherever possible for supplies, including the windows, cabinetry, drywall, concrete block, trusses, and metal work.

Given that the client was already living in the house, the design team were able to see how they used the space and identify points of improvement. It became clear that the client wanted a carefree, low-maintenance structure, with the option of accommodating large groups of people for entertaining. A key player throughout the design and construction process, the client's career as a writer provided a fresh perspective to the creative team.

The project became an exercise in taking the standard elements of the American ranch house idiom and reinterpreting them when necessary to form a house responsive to contemporary needs and priorities. Evoking much of the original structure's architecture, the house retains its community identity, allowing it to still serve as a social hub in the neighborhood.

Nestled on a beautiful 170-acre (69-hectare) property, along Porter Creek in rural Sonoma County, this off-the-grid homestead has been designed and constructed to ensure harmony with the surrounding landscape and minimal environmental impact. The indoor/outdoor flow creates an enriching and peaceful living space for the family and their deep appreciation for the natural world.

While the property offered several possible building sites, solar analysis led to a south-sloping open hillside. Much of the property is shaded by the ridge south of the creek, but has ample access to sun throughout the year. The western edge is tucked in and shaded by mature oak trees, which provide sun protection during summer afternoons. This site allowed the architects to route the driveway access further from the creek, eliminating the ranch road that had been channeling rainwater runoff into the creek.

The homestead is designed as a series of east-west running volumes, stepping up the hill and roughly paralleling the topography. Direct sunlight keeps the main living spaces warm during cooler months, while overhangs and exterior shade fins direct the summer sun away from windows during warmer months.

Arkin Tilt Architects

# HEALDSBERG RESIDENCE

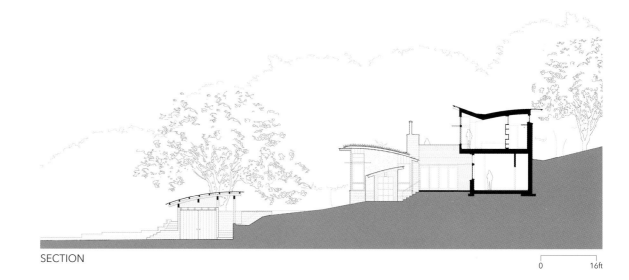

SECTION

0                    16ft

The kitchen transparently links these bars, with doors opening wide to a narrow contoured terrace, connecting the house with the pool. The pool house doubles as guest space, with the upper level used as an art and essential oil studio that faces the home's edible gardens.

The planted living room roof blends into the landscape while the other roofs, topped by gently curving corrugated metal, provide a softened take on typical agrarian structures and mimic the surrounding tree canopies. This residence exemplifies innovative sustainable design with its hybrid use of materials and site-sensitive building.

Designed for a couple who found themselves drawn back to the growing vibrancy and culture of the city, this home was designed to mimic the peace and quiet of their larger, previous home but on a smaller scale and specifically tailored to their tastes and activities. Located on the north edge of the Madison Valley neighborhood, the home abuts the fringe of the Washington Park Arboretum, but is within easy walking distance of the village center.

Early design discussions focused on a simple and modern structure, with a purity of materials and a quiet palette constructed on a modest budget. The couple desired a home that was open, light filled, and private but also transparent and open to views of the landscape. Above all, they described a quiet design integrated with the landscape to create a tangible calmness in the home. The concept grew from this premise, drawing complexity from the opportunities and constraints of an urban corner lot.

A courtyard in the center of the site brings light and private outdoor space deeper into the site, and serves as an organizational hub for the home. The sunnier south and western fringes of the site are reserved for gardens. Territorial view corridors helped identify where areas of transparency could work and where privacy was required.

Mw|works Architecture + Design

# HELEN STREET

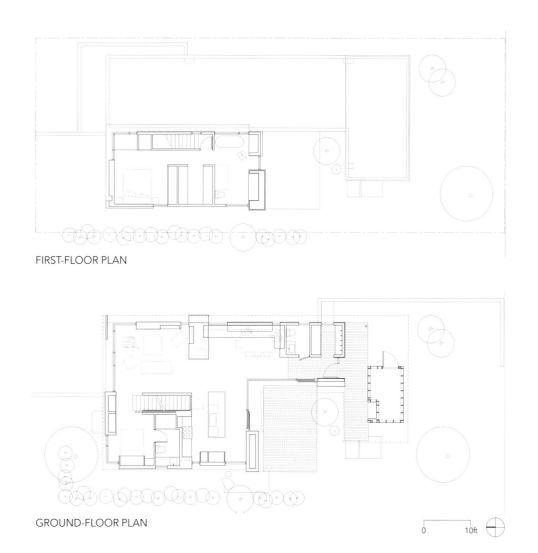

FIRST-FLOOR PLAN

GROUND-FLOOR PLAN

0        10ft

Location **Seattle, Washington** Area **2270 ft² (211 m²)** Completed **2015** Photography **Andrew Pogue**

The material palette was simple, with a largely glass-filled main level and solid volumes crisply detailed in cement panels. Floating above, the roof plane and master suite are clad in naturally weathered cedar planks. Anchoring the house around the courtyard, the outdoor chimney and garden shed are clad in heavy reclaimed timbers, stacked and blackened.

By working closely with the owner, who also managed and built the project, design concept and execution were closely integrated from concept through to fabrication. The limited construction budget was focused on key spaces and experiences, while other aspects were kept more straightforward. With a shared understanding of project goals there was a great economy of communication and efficiency in realizing the project.

The outcome is a home that is simple but very intentional, serving as a backdrop to the landscape and the lifestyle of its inhabitants.

Reimagined with a minimalist aesthetic, this project also honors and incorporates design cues from the home's original architect, Frank Gehry. In order to create an open-air plan and work/display space for the owner/artist, the first floor was gutted. Interiors have been arranged around an existing, oversized rectangular skylight, while new windows bring additional natural light into the kitchen and living areas. The architect created a dynamic undulating staircase wall that acts as sculptural statement within the home, emerging into an expressive and handcrafted walnut staircase.

A fish-scale, copper-clad entryway leads into a compressed vestibule, which introduces dominant themes throughout the home: white vertical planes and the concrete ground plane, both disrupted by walnut surfaces. The dynamic swoosh shape of the staircase wall captures light throughout the day, accentuating the golden tones of the wood as the slats encourage a dance of light and shadow.

Dan Brunn Architecture

# HIDE
# OUT

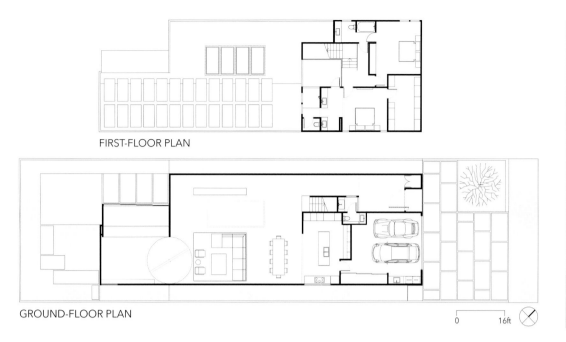

FIRST-FLOOR PLAN

GROUND-FLOOR PLAN

0        16ft

Location **Los Angeles, California** Area **3600 ft² (334 m²)** Completed **2016** Photography **Brandon Shigeta**

Minimal furnishings define 'rooms' within the open plan, allowing art to remain center stage. Adjacent to the living space is the dining area and kitchen. The all-white kitchen is serene, featuring white back-painted matte glass along built-in cabinets and drawers. Adding dimension to the all-white surfaces, the architect plays with material finishes to accentuate differences in utility. The cooking area looks onto the new garden through a frameless window, spanning from the countertop to ceiling. A pure white, Caesarstone kitchen island is sleek and elemental, and in conjunction with a similarly constructed wood dining table, carries on the home's minimalist aesthetic. At the far end of the house, a pivoting wall either hides or reveals a multi-purpose room.

Taking cues from Japanese teahouses, the architect designed a wooden box-like volume for a variety of activities. Upstairs, natural light seeps into the stairwell tunnel through a glass-enclosed, open-air meditative garden, accessible through the master bathroom. Previously boxed in with no access to the outdoors, the space was designed to acknowledge Gehry's original intention of making the area an encased greenhouse.

This extensive renovation and addition to an Edward Lutyens-inspired home sits on a wooded Hillsborough estate. The architects were posed with a unique design challenge: retain the timeless characters of the home's front façade, while accommodating additional and contemporary arrangements of space, which open up to an expansive backyard and new pool house. The solution was to unify the massing with a composition of simple peaked-roof volumes around a large glazed prism, with a metal-clad circulation spine to bridge the gap between the old and new styles.

The pool house was conceived as an intervention in the landscape. The simple, single-story massing, capped with a low-slope roof and clad in dry-stacked stone and extensive glazing, reads as an extension of the main home's lower façade. Lift-and-slide doors open fully to the poolside patio, capturing cooling breezes and creating an open-feel pavilion for dining and entertaining.

Studio VARA

# HILLSBOROUGH RESIDENCE

Hobby Barn is a thoughtful historic renovation and addition to an original Hiram Halle home built in 1880. The clients, a celebrated photographer and an avid art lover, wanted their weekend retreat to showcase their art collection as well as accommodate the needs of their growing children. To do this, the clients commissioned the architect to create a new sense of arrival to the house, incorporating a dramatic cantilevered steel-and-glass staircase as well as developing a second story for the clients' children to have a space of their own.

Fronted on a country road, the public side of the home reflects its historic character, including reuse of original Hiram Halle windows in the new façade. The rear elevation features modernist ribbons of glass, emphasizing the bucolic landscape beyond. In the newly designed entry foyer, the drama is heightened by a multi-layer chandelier made from repurposed industrial fixtures, hung from a suspended mounting plate and custom designed by the architect. A 'bridge' connecting to the other side of the house, which had been previously renovated, creates a link between the past and present. The existing concrete floor was painted barn red to incorporate the signature color found on all Hiram Halle properties.

Carol Kurth Architecture

# HOBBY BARN

GROUND-FLOOR PLAN

UPPER-LEVEL FLOOR PLAN

0        16ft

Location **Pound Ridge, New York** Area **3000 ft² (279 m²)** Completed **2014** Photography **Albert Vecerka/Esto**

Traditional barn materials such as steel, timber, and stone have been playfully incorporated as modern details, and expressed in the industrial aesthetic of the glass-and-steel staircase that floats through the space. Sliding barn doors on exposed-steel tracks further emphasize the industrial barn motif, and echo the home's origins.

The newly revitalized space has a cool, relaxed feel of a weekend country home with the refined feel of a modern gallery.

203

Nestled into the hillside of a Santa Monica canyon, this home's activities and views organize themselves along a defined path through outdoor and open interior spaces. The property's entry procession descends through an impromptu, landscaped amphitheater, then bends to reveal framed glimpses of the canyon below. Looking through the home from its front door entrance, the exterior beyond is offset and revealed by a large, telescoping glass wall. A long skylight extends and continues along the entry path as it winds through the living spaces, illuminating the home with bright but indirect light. As the skylight bends, it creates distinctions between the kitchen, living, and dining areas, while visually linking the front and back entrances. Courtyards created by the structural form are likewise connected by the high skylight-sculpted ceilings overhead. The home's cross section is punctuated by the same winding light that slips to further distinguish these living areas, shaping their individual volumes subtly within the whole.

## Griffin Enright Architects

# HOLLANDER RESIDENCE

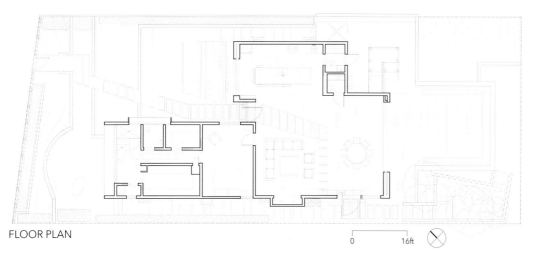

FLOOR PLAN

0   16ft

At the rear façade, pocket doors disappear to frame the view of the exterior from the living room. A deck at the rear looks back on the living area and through the house to the front courtyard. A raised ceiling in the main-living area complements the view from the back courtyard. As the ceiling lifts, it echoes the entry court's descending sequence of steps and slope. The house is both held together as a whole, and divided into parts by the volumetric carving of the skylight. The exterior seems to pull through the house along the same path, as the visual continuity between the back and front courtyards is maintained along the home's zigzag spine.

Location **Santa Monica, California** Area **1900 ft² (177 m²)** Completed **2014** Photography **Timothy Street-Porter**

Door County is a peninsula jutting into Lake Michigan known for spectacular views, limestone cliffs, and agriculture fields. The number of farmsteads in the area has reduced over time but many weathered pine-sided barns still exist. Those that remain have a memorable quality to their stature.

This single-family residence addresses the vernacular architecture of the area with its steep-pitched steel roof, naturally aging cedar siding, lean-to in the rear, and composition of square windows. The white trim surrounding the windows and white fences complement the naturally ageing materials. The base of the exterior is clad in a black paper and resin, and maintenance-free richlite material to protect the longevity of the cedar siding.

The orientation of the building, situated among native grasses and evergreens, is east-west for optimal light gain. White wood fences emphasize the parking area and the home's entrance pathway. The interior finishes are simple and clean: white drywall, pine wood floors, and bright color accents. The kitchen is fresh with white casework and stone countertops highlighted by a blue-tile splashback.

Salmela Architects

# HOUSE FOR BETH

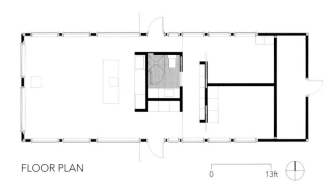

FLOOR PLAN

0           13ft

Location **Door County, Wisconsin** Area **973 ft² (90 m²)** Completed **2015** Photography **Paul Crosby**

Located in the northern suburbs of Chicago, this house sits opposite the unique 135-foot (13-meter) high Baha'i Temple. Made of white stone, the structure is symmetrically spherical and monumental.

The street-side face of the house needed to negotiate not only the scale and specificity of its unusual neighboring architecture but also the eclectic nature of the suburban environment. It also required a 40-foot (4-meter) differential elevation between the road and the lake.

The house consists of four levels, with a two-story structure, windowless on the street, containing the garage, gym, and guest suite. This façade is un-residential in scale, but prevents imposition of the monument it faces. Almost an inversion of the grand stairs opposite, which lead to the temple's entrance, the home's main entrance is located at the top of a set of stairs, with the spaces of the house slowly revealed on the way down to the beach below. On descending the processional, light-filled stairway the house gives itself away beneath the suburban lawn above. Moving down and through the home encourages a mental landscape and creates an architectural experience through which the structure is gradually pieced together in its entirety.

The home achieves a transition from suburban streets to lakeside beach on an unusual site. From the working world to family life, from formal to informal, from public to private, it is a place of overlapping journeys.

GLUCK+

# HOUSE TO THE BEACH

Location **Chicago, Illinois** Area **14,500 ft² (1347 m²)** Completed **2015** Photography **Paul Warchol**

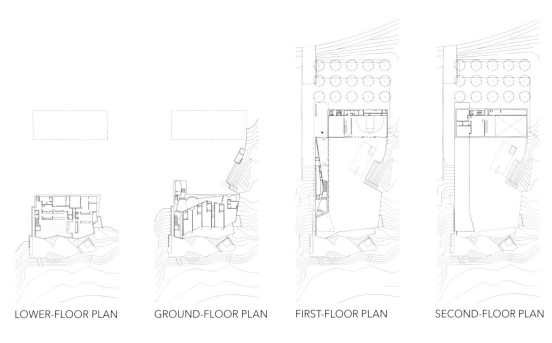

LOWER-FLOOR PLAN     GROUND-FLOOR PLAN     FIRST-FLOOR PLAN     SECOND-FLOOR PLAN     0   40ft

This Northern Minnesota cabin replaces an old uninsulated structure. It was shifted from its original orientation toward the lake at the east of the existing cabin. This longer plan faces south and looks toward the restored cinder-block sauna. Shifting the orientation allowed the home's east end to be fully glazed and without visual obstruction. It also provided the opportunity for a south-facing deck and welcome entry under the cantilevered second floor.

The master bedroom is on the first floor with the two guest rooms on the upper level. A workshop iunder this main floor and includes a terrace beneath the cantilever. A new boathouse flanks the fireplace terrace at the shoreline.

The all-wood interior has been locally supplied. The exterior is stained with a pine tar-like treatment and a splash base has been installed below the wood siding to ensure its longevity. The dry-laid stone walls, steps, and pathways provide a wonderful warmth and contextual appropriateness to the rugged Northern Minnesota setting.

Salmela Architects

# HYYTINEN CABIN

GROUND-FLOOR PLAN         FIRST-FLOOR PLAN         SECOND-FLOOR PLAN      0     10ft

Location **Lake Vermilion, Minnesota** Area **2144 ft² (199 m²)** Completed **2015** Photography **Paul Crosby**

Situated on a small island between mainland Miami and North Miami Beach, this home was designed to capture, filter, and reflect the surrounding water, radiant tropical sun, and meditative moon.

Careful reading of the site—with its expansive views of Biscayne Bay and the play of light from the water, sun, and moon—resulted in a house conceived as a series of pavilions interlaced with lush gardens, water elements, and shaded pathways. Each pavilion is enclosed with louvers and delicately veiled by large glass windows.

Stone walls create a sense of permanence, luxury, and timeless modernity. The walls create direction through the project and dissolve gently into ever-present gardens. A layering of materials, both porous and opaque, results in light controlled by the architecture, thereby delivering orchestrated compositions of vivid light and shadow patterns. Reflecting pools flow from the outdoor gardens to indoor living spaces, blurring boundaries between interior and exterior. Within the house, materials take on a canvas-like quality, reflecting variations of light.

The pavilions wrap around tropical courtyard spaces and open onto a pool, a lawn planted with eco-friendly peanut grass, and a small private sand beach. Moving through the site, spaces unravel and intertwine while maintaining a constant visual connection with the open sky and waterfront.

Rene Gonzalez Architect

# INDIAN CREEK RESIDENCE

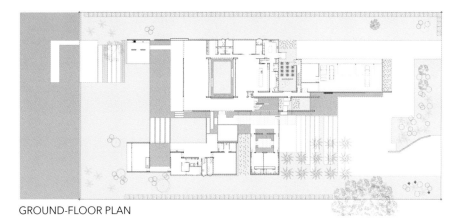

GROUND-FLOOR PLAN

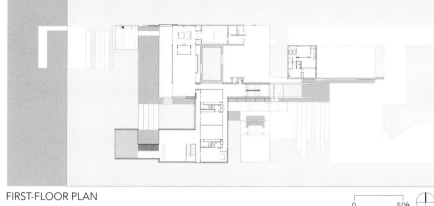

FIRST-FLOOR PLAN

0    50ft

Location **Miami, Florida** Area **20,000 ft² (1858 m²)** Completed **2014** Photography **Michael Stavaridis, Luis Ravieso**

Designed for a couple interested in simplifying their lives and learning to live with less, this home was created with a holistic and sustainable approach to architectural design.

The home's spaces evoke a sense of completeness, eliminating the desire to accumulate 'things.' The simple, efficient and quiet design is a reaction to today's technology and offers a refuge in an ever-changing, chaotic world.

The house is located on a tree-filled site in an area once rich in fishing and logging, and still supported by a commuter ferry. It is respectful to the existing landscape and makes minimal contact with the ground, complementing its surroundings rather than competing against them. To honor the existing site, all of the trees were left in place and excess excavation limited to protect tree roots, leaving only 18 feet (2 meters) in width and 80 feet (7 meters) in length for the house. Trees and water surround the house and instead of implementing typical design solutions with unobstructed views of the water, the central tree is visually dominant. Vistas are accentuated through blocking and slowly revealing views, creating a journey to the water.

Suyama Peterson Deguchi

# THE JUNSEI HOUSE

A modern interpretation of the classic Hawaii summer camp, this warm and spacious home was designed with longevity in mind. Incorporating various timeless elements, which remain relevant to century-old architecture and design, the architects intended to create a home that would aesthetically stand the test of time.

In reference to traditional Hawaiian architecture, the home is made up of multiple communal hangout spots, allowing for interaction among residents and guests. Located at the base of the Big Island's large cinder cone, Pu'u Ku'ili, it offers expansive views of the Pacific Ocean and Kua Bay, as well as mountain views of Hualalai. The property was originally used for ranching and the owners felt compelled to return it to its natural state with the re-naturalization of a collapsed lava tube and bunch grasses. Furthermore, the buildings reinforce the camp-like aesthetic by utilizing simple, durable materials such as board-formed concrete, western red cedar, oversized sliding doors, operable wood ventilation louvers, and rope lashing.

The commodious and open backyard includes a large overhang of western red cedar, which shelters a tiki bar and cozy sitting area. This space, complete with multiple lounge chairs and breathtaking ocean views, spills over into the pool. A barbeque/luau area allows for gatherings of family and friends under the comfort and shade of a kiawe tree.

Walker Warner Architects

# KAHUA KUILI

SITE PLAN

0    50ft

Location **Big Island, Hawaii** Area **4500 ft² (418 m²)** Completed **2013** Photography **Matthew Millman**

Marion Philpotts of Philpotts Interiors incorporated bright colors and retro elements, tying into the modern theme of the structure, while creating a vintage vibe. The expansive kitchen constructed in western red cedar includes a breakfast bar, dining table, and state-of-the-art appliances. Its tall ceiling, large windows, and grand sliding doors, which open to the backyard, are cohesive with the open and airy theme of the house. Intimate spaces for privacy are implemented throughout the home, including cozy reading nooks and relaxing sitting areas. It is the perfect place to unwind and enjoy the natural climate and landscape of Hawaii.

Perched above Kauna'oa Bay on Hawaii's Big Island is Kauhale Kai. Inspiration for the home came from the client's affinity for modern art and architecture, along with their desire to capture Hawaii's warm sense of *aloha* in a seaside home to share with extended family.

The resulting interpretation of the traditional, close-knit, Hawaiian *kauhale* (settlement) is an enhanced version of the island's laid-back style, driven by restraint and understatement but designed for tropical livability.

Seven separate pavilions are organized around an architectural pool, which acts the home's axis. Outdoor garden spaces serve as corridors linking the pavilions or hales and creating a village-like atmosphere. These transitional spaces add a gracious quality to the home and provide a unifying synergy between the hale structures, tropical plantings, large-scale stone exterior elements, and the site's coastal views.

de Reus Architects

# KAUHALE KAI

Minimalist finishes reinforce the home's clean lines, with warm woods complementing cool sand-grained plaster and brushed travertine floors and walls.

Easily maintained finishes and floors that welcome bare feet reinforce the *aloha* factor. Coral stone columns supporting hipped-roof pavilions—island architecure at its most elemental—are encased by steel-and-glass doors.

Location **Kohala, Hawaii** Area **6700 ft² (2042 m²)** Completed **2011** Photography **Joe Fletcher**

SITE PLAN

0          50ft

A common thread in the design of (fer) studio's work is to create an integrated space by responding to existing conditions with new approaches to design. When all aspects of the project are equally engaged, a transformative space emerges, creating a codependency between what remains and what is built new. The approach to this residence, cognizant of cost and scope, focused on the middle portion of the original 1950s, single-storey, ranch-style home and its relationship as a spatial link in the development of new living, dining, and kitchen areas as well as the master bedroom suite.

In addition, the magnificent natural conditions of the site–its sloping terrain, large redwoods, dappled sunlight, and overall wooded atmosphere–were the inspirational element behind setting up day lighting views along the axis.

As a result, the existing house was opened up through the center running in the east/west direction, engaging the house to the landscape. Overall, the new design links the front entry experience, first to the core of the house, and then spatially extends it out to the rear yard/deck, and on to the lower rear yard/pool, originally completely discounted from the house.

Christopher Mercier, (fer) studio

# KIM RESIDENCE

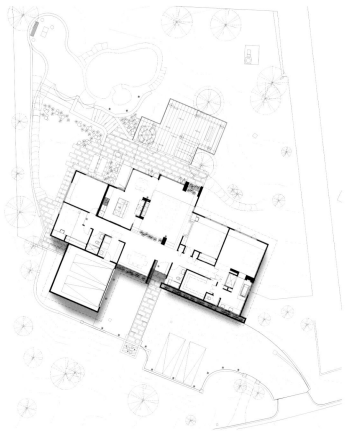

FLOOR PLAN

0          16ft

In many ways the completed home enhances the positive features of the original house. It does so by first envisioning these conditions as opportunities, and secondly, by further developing them in a more architecturally significant and sustainably responsible manner. In conjunction with furniture and fixtures chosen by Sarah Buxton Design, the new house—owned by CEO of Hana Financial, Sunnie Kim—transforms into a contemporary living experience, engaging both interior and exterior spaces in a continuous living environment.

Laid out during the Florida land boom of the 1920s, the Las Olas section of Fort Lauderdale is characterized by a network of interlacing canals branching off Las Olas Boulevard, west of the Intracoastal Waterway. Over the past few decades most of the neighborhood's relatively modest original bungalows and villas have been replaced by larger and more elaborate houses in an array of styles, ranging from Venetian Gothic to Caribbean to Modernist.

The design of this villa, on a site at the intersection of a major and subsidiary canal, is rooted in the more human-scaled, unprepossessing architecture of the area's earlier development. As with many early twentieth-century Mediterranean Revival homes—and the Andalusian farmhouses that inspired them—this house is composed of simple, discrete volumes juxtaposed for anecdotal effect. The sinuous plan opens oblique distant views across the two waterways from the main rooms, while loggias and galleries alongside a walled garden buffer the house from neighbors and the street. Local symmetries at each façade help to formally define the landscaped 'rooms' immediately adjacent to them, establishing a hierarchy of scale commensurate with the size of the house, without compromising its picturesque quality.

Robert A. M. Stern Architects, Roger H. Seifter, Partner

# LAS OLAS

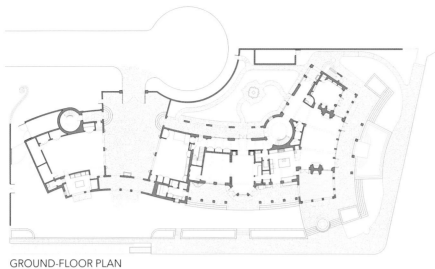

GROUND-FLOOR PLAN

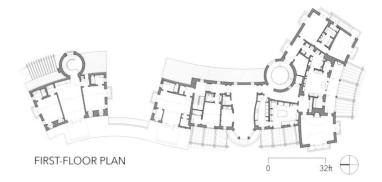

FIRST-FLOOR PLAN

0        32ft

Architectural detailing inside and out is informal and subdued, despite its complexity and intricacy. The material palette—limited to plaster, wood, tile, stone, and iron—is either reclaimed or convincingly antiqued, and subtly varied from room to room, while colors throughout the house are muted. As a result, the house has an air of calm and sobriety, and is rooted to its place.

Designed as a home and studio for a photographer and his young family, Lightbox is located on a peninsula that extends south from British Columbia, across the border to Point Roberts. The densely forested site lies beside a 180-acre (73-hectare) park that overlooks the Strait of Georgia, the San Juan Islands and Puget Sound.

Having experienced the world from under a black focusing cloth and through a large format camera lens, the owner has a fondness for simplicity and an appreciation of unique, genuine, and well-crafted details.

The home was made decidedly modest, in size and means, with a building skin utilizing simple materials in a straightforward yet innovative configuration. Exposed wood two-bys form a structural frame and directly support a prefabricated aluminum window system of standard glazing units, uniformly sized to reduce the complexity and overall cost.

Bohlin Cywinski Jackson

# LIGHTBOX

This home is nestled into a lush second-growth forest on a north-facing bluff, overlooking the Hood Canal with distant views of Dabob Bay. Designed to repurpose an existing foundation, the new building is just over 398 square feet (27 square meters). The simple form is abstracted against the forest surrounds, with its stark exterior contrasting a warm bright interior.

The owners live full-time in Houston but have shared many summers with family at a nearby property outside Seabeck. They loved the wildness of the southern canal and imagined a small retreat here of their own. Early design discussions focused on creating a compact, modern structure that was simple and efficient to build. Intentionally restrained on an existing footprint, the concept grew from this premise. A simple box with large carved openings in both the roof and walls selectively embraces views and natural light.

Visitors approach the site from the south. A thin canopy marks the entry and frames views of the canal below. The more transparent north and west elevations pull the landscape and distant view into the space.

Mw|works Architecture + Design

# LITTLE HOUSE

GROUND-FLOOR PLAN

FIRST-FLOOR PLAN

0          10ft

With primary views toward the water, the south and east elevations remain mostly solid, shielding views from the driveway and neighboring properties. Skylights have been carved into the roof, bringing light and views of the stars over the bed and into the shower.

Taut oxidized black cedar and blackened cement infill panels clad the exterior, while lightly painted MDF panels and soft pine plywood warm and brighten the interior. On the sunny western corner of the home a large patio reaches out into the landscape and connects the building to the larger site, while serving as a descent point to the trail system wandering down to the water's edge.

The small footprint served as an effective tool in governing the design process. Focus was placed on the essentials, and extras were edited out by both desire and necessity. The resulting project hopes to capture the essence of the modern cabin—small in size but much larger than its boundaries.

This single-family residence is a modernist reinterpretation of the Northern California ranch-style home. Designed around an existing Japanese maple tree—a vestige of the previous landscape and the relationship shared between residence and site—the house takes full advantage of the Silicon Valley's mild climate. While windows and doors fill interiors with air and light, they also frame views of the diverse flora surrounding the home. In the living room a wall of sliding glass doors blurs the line between indoors and out. In the master bedroom, one can hear the trickling of water and quiet rustling of trees coming from the meditation garden just outside. It is these moments that help anchor the building to site.

The main house is composed of a central, double-height living and communal space, which runs parallel to the street, shielding the home from the quiet thoroughfare. This common area, which includes a modest kitchen and place for family gathering, connects two single-story volumes, each containing a variety of private and functional spaces. Outside a linear pool and board-formed concrete garden wall, located along the eastern edge of the property, visually connect the main building to the guesthouse beyond.

Bohlin Cywinski Jackson

# LOS ALTOS RESIDENCE

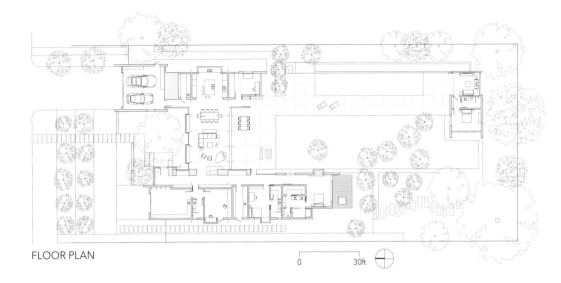

FLOOR PLAN

0   30ft

Location **Los Altos, California** Area **Main: 4151 ft² (386 m²) Guest: 479 ft² (45 m²)** Completed **2015** Photography **Nic Lehoux**

The home is detailed with a natural, crisp palette, reflecting the client's fondness for simplicity and tranquility. A variety of woods, including Douglas fir, western red cedar, and gray elm, have been used throughout and provide a sense of warmth directly contrasted by exposed structural steel, polished concrete floors, and a textured concrete fireplace. Designed to be environmentally conscious, the home has sustainable measures. This includes passive cooling; renewable energy; thermal massing; indoor air quality; energy conservation methods, such as polyurethane and fiberglass blow-in insulation; and water reduction strategies, including low-flow plumbing fixtures and zone-drip irrigation.

The simple layout and detailing of this single-story residence, with its numerous connections to the surrounding landscape, creates a home that is both calm and restful for the family to enjoy for many years to come.

A renovation and structural addition brought what was a well conceived but poorly realized mid-century home to its full potential.

A contemporary version of the translucent cast-glass window was added at the opposing end of the home's entry as a companion piece to the original. Made of hot-rolled steel, with a laser-cut perforated wave pattern and changeable LED lamps, its characteristics are carried into the home and echoed in the Momoko Sudo's *in situ* painting, which adorns the living-room wall.

Sliding frameless glass panels between the kitchen and dining, and dining and family room create a strong sense of internal translucence. Custom-cast concrete tiles have been introduced to the entry, living room, and view terrace, creating a seamless transition to the home's exterior.

Hot-rolled steel has been used to enhance the two existing fireplaces and a steel hearth in the family-room fireplace has been sculpted to form steps up to the laundry and guest-bedroom wing of the house; a design feature that takes on a purely sculptural form when the hidden, coplanar wood door is closed. Reclaimed eucalyptus, felled at the Presidio of San Francisco, has been used on all of the cabinetry wood veneer in the kitchen area and family room.

Mark English Architects

# LOS GATOS RESIDENCE

SITE PLAN

0      40ft

Location **Los Gatos, California** Area **3704 ft² (344m²)** Completed **2016** Photography **Joe Fletcher**

Marcheeta is located on a tight lot in the hills above Sunset Strip, Los Angeles. The main design goals for the project were to take advantage of the view, utilize the site topography to create space for a large lower-level entertainment area and garage, and create privacy from the street.

The sloping nature of the lot also allowed the creation of a small rear yard. The lower-level entertainment space opens onto a pleasant courtyard containing a fire pit and water feature, which also gives light and access to secondary bedrooms. A beautiful marble wall screening a quiet courtyard opens to the kitchen and resolves privacy from the street.

Large operable walls of glass and linear skylights flood the home with natural light. A warm, rich palette of natural wood and stone, created in collaboration with interior designer Lynda Murray, gives the home a comfortable and elegant feel. A unique feature of the home is the pool on the main level, which cascades into main water feature wrapping around the fire pit. The pool also contains skylights that filter daylight and views of passing swimmers to the gym below.

## McClean Design

# MARCHEETA

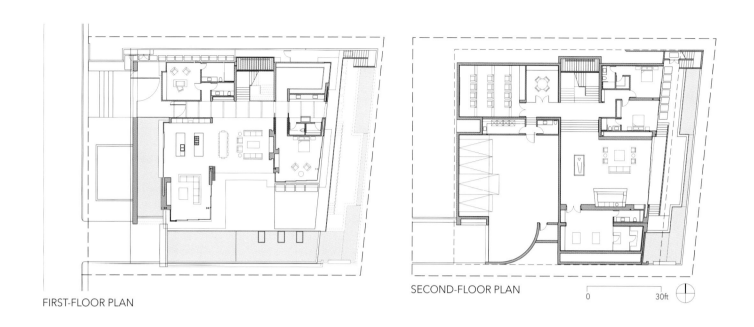

FIRST-FLOOR PLAN

SECOND-FLOOR PLAN

0       30ft

Location **Los Angeles, California** Area **9000 ft² (836 m²)** Completed **2016** Photography **Jim Barstch**

Carefully placed in a copse of trees at the easterly end of a large meadow, this home has two major building volumes. A grounded two-story bedroom wing anchors a raised living pavilion, which is lifted off the ground by a series of exposed steel columns. Visible from the access road, the large meadow in front of the house continues beneath the main living space, transforming it into a bridge-like structure. The raised floor level provides enhanced views and prevents winter snow accumulation—typical of the upper Methow Valley— in the home's main living area.

To emphasize the idea of lightness, the living pavilion roof changes pitch along its length, warping upwards at each end. The exposed interior wood beams appear like an unfolding fan as the roof pitch changes. The main interior bearing columns are steel with a tapered V shape.

The home is a reflection of the architects' continuing investigation into the idea of crafted modernism with cast-bronze inserts at the front door, variegated laser-cut steel railing panels, a curvilinear cast-glass kitchen counter, waterjet-cut aluminum light fixtures, and many custom furniture pieces. The interior has been designed to integrate completely with the exterior.

FINNE Architects

# MAZAMA HOUSE

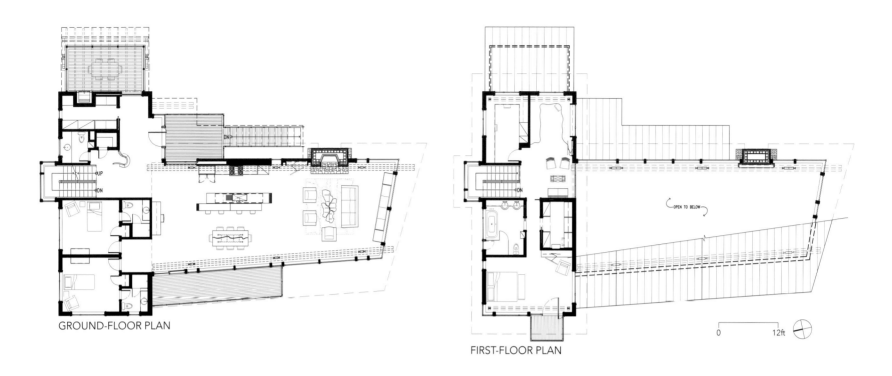

GROUND-FLOOR PLAN

FIRST-FLOOR PLAN

OPEN TO BELOW

0        12ft

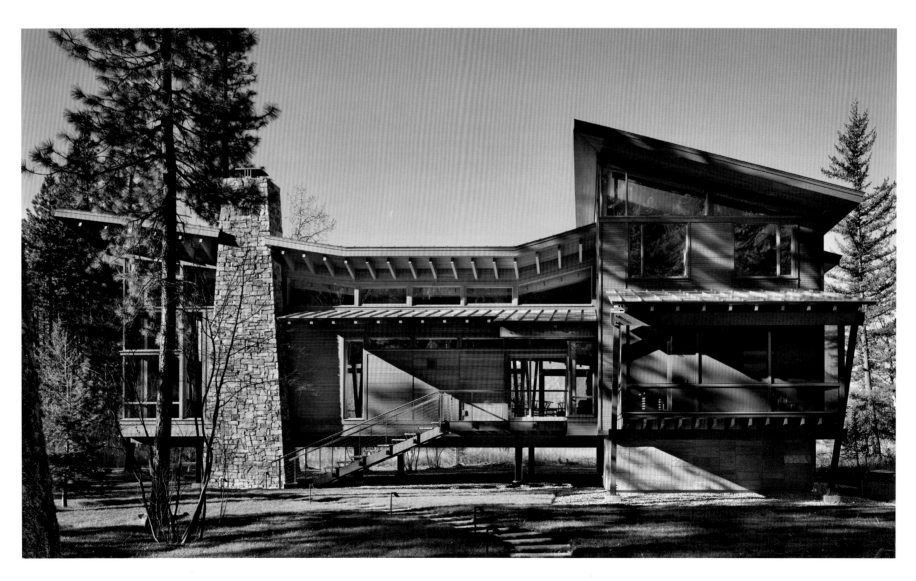

Designed from the beginning as a sustainable structure, the home includes 40 percent higher insulation values than required by code, radiant concrete slab heating, efficient natural ventilation, large amounts of natural lighting, water-conserving plumbing fixtures, and locally sourced materials. Windows have high-performance Low-E insulated glazing and concealed shades. A radiant, hydronic heat system with exposed concrete floors allows lower operating temperatures and higher occupant comfort levels. The concrete slabs conserve heat and provide great warmth and comfort throughout the home. Deep roof overhangs, built-in shades and high operating clerestory windows have been used to reduce heat gain in summer months. During the winter, the lower sun angle penetrates into living spaces, passively warming the exposed concrete floor. Low VOC paints and stains have been used throughout the house. The high level of craft evident in this project reflects another key principle of sustainable design: build it well so it lasts for many years.

Location **Methow Valley, Washington** Area **4400 ft² (408 m²)** Completed **2015** Photography **Benjamin Benschneider**

This home is located on a former hunting and fishing preserve oriented around three glacial lakes. The landscape is characterized by dense forests and rocky outcroppings, as well as the various estates designed by prominent architects at the turn of the nineteenth century.

The site is defined by two massive granite escarpments and metered by a series of retaining walls quarried on site, echoing the historic stone walls prevalent throughout Tuxedo Park. The design celebrates the extreme topography of the site, which defines the sectional development of the house. The site design controls the flow of water, diverting runoff to the east of the house into series of water terraces, allowing it to be filtered through a sequence of gardens before reaching Tuxedo Lake.

Three enclosed living levels and a sequence of outdoor terraces have been organized in an ascending route. The lower level includes a garden room and exterior entry courtyard. An exterior stepped ramp rises to the main entry level, which includes a foyer, library, and guest bedroom.

WEISS/MANFREDI Architecture/Landscape/Urbanism

# MCCANN RESIDENCE

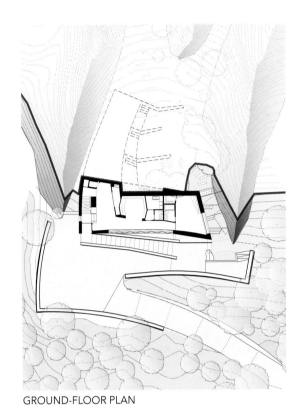

GROUND-FLOOR PLAN

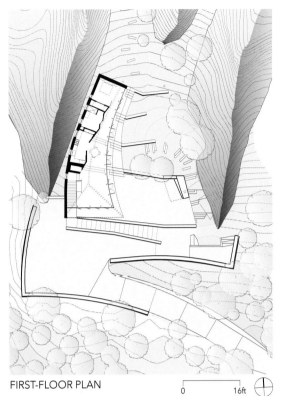

FIRST-FLOOR PLAN

0          16ft

Location **Tuxedo Park, New York** Area **4800 ft² (446 m²)** Completed **2014** Photography  **Albert Vecerka/Esto, Jeff Goldberg/Etso**

A double-height stair hall connects the main level to the upper garden level—a loft-like glass pavilion with panoramic vistas of Tuxedo Lake. This level features a sequence of platforms for living, kitchen, and dining, and a master bedroom. The terraced gardens create open-air 'rooms' defined by the arc of the house and the granite outcropping.

The design features a material palette noted for its ability to weather over time. Custom bronze screens filter light and maximize privacy. Granite walls, mined from a nearby quarry, have been constructed from the same stone as the escarpment. Blurring the connection between landscape and architecture, this home embraces its historic setting by introducing a new inhabitable topography.

Designed for a couple and their two sons, this home is nestled at the end of a cul-de-sac with spectacular views of the Pacific Ocean. Upon entry, along a 50-foot-long (15-meter-long) teak-clad wall, the home opens spectacularly out to ocean views and the Southern California climate.

The challenge was to provide gracious and open living spaces despite the restrictive 11-foot (3-meter) height limit imposed by the homeowners association. The solution was to create a series of horizontally expansive spaces underneath a floating horizontal plane, supported by stone masses, wood walls, and slender steel columns. Oversized sliding glass doors retract completely, dissolving physical boundaries between the interior and the exterior, creating an uninterrupted flow. An enclosed central courtyard provides additional space to enjoy the mild climate, and serves as an outdoor living room.

Ehrlich Yanai Rhee Chaney Architects

# MCELROY RESIDENCE

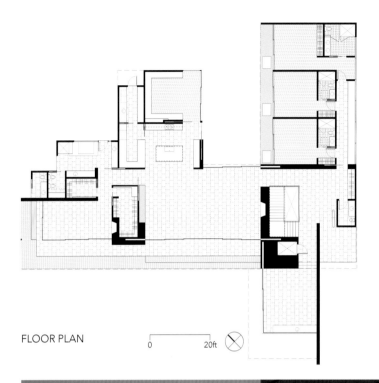

FLOOR PLAN

0        20ft

The master suite enjoys a layered view over the swimming pool and ocean. The master bathroom opens onto its own private meditative garden nestled in between the house and topography behind. A home office, guest and children's bedrooms open onto a protected central courtyard, which features an outdoor kitchen, dining area, and koi pond. A garage, health room, and storage/service areas are all located in the basement, freeing up the entire ground plane for living. The stone floor has been extended outside, along with a composition of teak, concrete, and landscaped area to provide a variety of outdoor entertaining and living areas.

Location **Laguna Beach, California** Area **7500 ft² (697 m²)** Completed **2014**
Photography **Miranda Boller/Photekt, Nico Marques/Photekt, Roger Davies**

This seasonal home for a family of four has been crafted with lasting materials and designed to capture maximum views, light, and prevailing winds of its surrounding meadow and beach landscape. The result distills the New England Victorian beachside cottage and introduces a Scandinavian sensibility to the casual context of Martha's Vineyard.

To blend in with its surroundings, the house is sided in the region's typical cedar shingles, and the massing is broken down into different volumes to appear more settled in the landscape. The primary gesture arranges the house in two volumes connected by a bridge, with an additional volume, the garage, placed in the front yard to minimize the home's generous scale within its half-acre site.

The articulated footprint is the result of multiple volumes perceived as appendages and voids, which express the interior room programs and layouts. Quiet yet dynamic, the beach cottage climbs and spreads across the site, animated by its own shadows and reflections.

Andrew Franz Architect

# MEADOW BEACH HOUSE

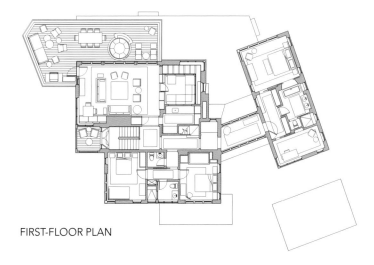

FIRST-FLOOR PLAN

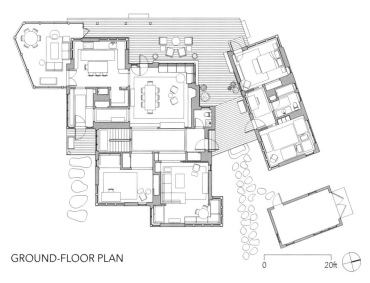

GROUND-FLOOR PLAN

0          20ft

Location **Martha's Vineyard, Massachusetts** Area **5000 ft² (465 m²)** Completed **2016** Photography **Albert Vecerka/Esto**

The entry sequence reveals a semi-inverted plan: the living room is upstairs with an outdoor deck, typical of Vineyard homes, to capture views. Elevated above the sandy soil, the entry and eastern rooms hover above a sunken living space, allowing them to capture the stunning western views. Five porches, covered and open, and an irregular floor plan with plenty of nooks and alcoves allow summer inhabitants to find their sun or shade at any time of day.

Inside, the home plays on woods in neutral tones, soft greys, and pale whites to respond to the ever-changing island light. Bolder finishes on the main floor give way to receding hues and fabrics upstairs. The copper and brass, summery ginghams, bright ceramics, and textured glass enliven the bright home, embracing the spirit of a vintage heirloom residence.

285

Perched on a woodland bluff overlooking Lake Michigan, this home has been designed as three offset structures. The first 'gathering' structure contains the living room, kitchen, and covered vista-seating terrace. The other two 'sleeping' structures contain the master bedroom suite and three children's bedrooms. A dining-area breezeway connects all three structures.

The roof scape has gentle undulations, which follow the movement of surrounding terrain, making a playful reference to the local vernacular architecture. The resulting rhythm of exposed-wood beams provides layers of asymmetrical vaults throughout the interiors while simultaneously expressing the structural integrity of the home. Custom scuppers are located at the valley of each roof and direct water off the structure and into irrigation drywells.

At the southern end of the house, a 20-foot (6-meter) cantilevered roof extends over the vista terrace, providing a vast, protected, and unobstructed view of the lake and surrounding woodlands. This terrace allows the residents to easily transition between indoors and outdoors for entertaining. A double-sided Corten fireplace evokes a sense of drama in the living room and terrace area.

Desai Chia Architecture, Environment Architects

# MICHIGAN LAKE HOUSE

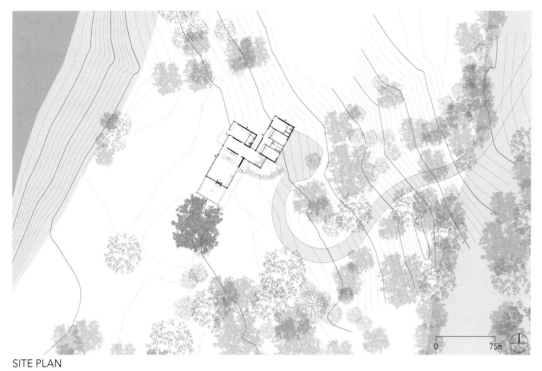
SITE PLAN

The home's exterior is clad in *shou sugi ban* cypress. *Shou sugi ban* is the traditional Japanese method of charring wood in order for it to become rot and insect resistant. The charred texture and deeply modulated façade members enhance shadows across the front of the home as the sun rises and sets.

Dying ash trees were reclaimed from the site, milled down, and used as the interior cabinetry, flooring, ceiling panels, and trim work. Ash wood was also incorporated in a series of custom furniture pieces, including a dining table, coffee tables, and bed for the master bedroom. The home's interiors have a direct connection to the indigenous landscape, which was once thriving with old growth ash.

Landscape design strategies were closely tied to the design of the home. A tight palette of native vegetation highlights views while also managing storm water runoff, and locally sourced stone creates outdoor seating areas, paths, and stairways.

Location **Michigan** Area **4800 ft² (446 m²)** Completed **2016** Photography **Paul Warchol**

Home to an Oscar-winning film and television producer, this project transformed an existing 1980s house into a light-filled, modern space. Since the original house was already well situated in its orientation to canyon views, the architects kept the building footprint in place and preserved the height and steep pitch of the roof to create a loft feeling inside.

From a forecourt, flanked by the screening room and three-car garage, a bridge spanning a reflecting pool grants access to the house. The home's interiors are organized to provide views and seamless access to outdoor spaces. A hallway extends across the entire breadth of the house from the foyer at the west to a covered porch at the east, which incorporates an outdoor kitchen. Most of the ground-floor rooms open directly to a limestone-paved patio at the rear, overlooking the swimming pool and golf course below the property. To highlight the owner's extensive art collection, the architects designed the interiors as clean-lined, flowing spaces open to views through floor-to-ceiling windows.

Rios Clementi Hale Studios

# MODERN BARN HOUSE

GROUND-FLOOR PLAN

FIRST-FLOOR PLAN

In addition to the home, a small guest house on the property was renovated into an artist's studio. A new swimming pool, limestone-paved patios, covered porches, tree swing, and yoga platform serve as additional places on the estate to unwind and relax. The screening room is cleverly sited at the front of the property, separated from the living space by the garage, to maintain privacy. Complementary slate-roof tiles and tongue-and-groove siding of gray-painted cedar replace the original exterior materials. New expanses of glass are screened from direct sunlight by a rhythmic pattern of vertical, aluminum fins, which form a continuous, two-story *brise soleil*. Large cantilevered windows rimmed in steel project from gabled additions on the north and south sides of the house, engaging the landscape. Original masonry chimneys were rebuilt to current seismic standards and hidden internal gutters maintain the home's taut profile. The resulting design reinterprets the traditional barn vernacular through modern simplicity and transparency.

Location **Los Angeles, California** Area **12,000 ft² (1115 m²)** Completed **2014** Photography **John Ellis**

Set on the stunning coastline of Greenwich, Connecticut, this modern shoreline colonial home features whitewashed handmade bricks, painted mahogany doors and windows, and beautifully finished interiors.

The stone-paved motor court was constructed with antique pavers salvaged during the restoration of Boston's Longfellow Bridge. Inside, the dining room ceiling has been assembled with rift-sawn oak purlins and planks, creating a contemporary version of a carved wooden palazzo ceiling. The floors are repurposed oak, with some rooms featuring a herringbone pattern. Fireplaces throughout the home are transitional, traditional, and all sourced from the United Kingdom.

An open-flow kitchen, breakfast room, and family room each boast water views, while a separate entrance leads into a mudroom, complete with heated bluestone floors. Spacious and open, the master bathroom features a four-directional vaulted ceiling and stenciled wood floor and bathtub, which has been placed under a large arched window to catch gorgeous views of the surrounding landscape.

Wadia Associates

# MODERN SHORELINE COLONIAL

Location **Greenwich, Connecticut** Area **8000 ft² (743 m²)** Completed **2016** Photography **Jonathan Wallen**

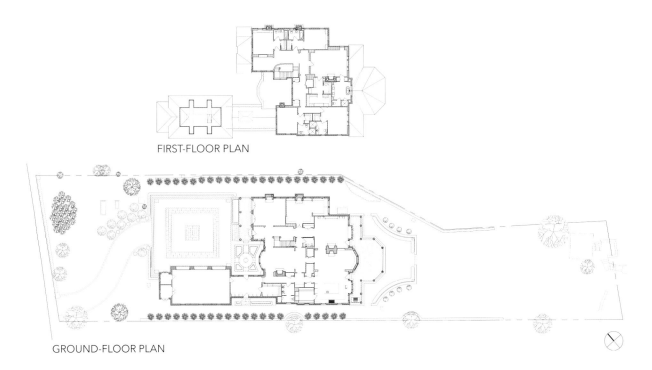

FIRST-FLOOR PLAN

GROUND-FLOOR PLAN

The finished basement contains a game, room, gym, massage room, and wine cellar. The back porch extends the entire width of the house and is equipped with motorized roll-down screens, while across the lawn toward the water is a pavilion, located close to the boat dock.

With the needs of a young family in mind, tasteful fabrics and paints were selected to stand the test of time without sacrificing beauty and style. A muted palette paired with a selection of complementary marble and tile has been used throughout, maintaining light throughout the home.

This project is an extensive remodel of an existing residence located on a severe hillside site overlooking the Pacific Ocean. The existing mid-century post-and-beam home required a structural, programmatic, and environmental upgrade, which resulted in a residence re-envisioned for the twenty-first century

The geometry of the existing roof was accentuated to create a language of faceted surfaces. The articulated volume of the building's front façade continues indoors, defining interior spaces. A blurring of the roof, wall, and floor planes occurs creating a forced perspective and framing extraordinary views of the Santa Monica Bay.

The minimal, gallery-like living space has been designed to accommodate the client's extensive contemporary art collection. Display niches, lighting, and the configuration of spaces are designed to enhance the experience of viewing the art. A steel stair with a custom laser-cut pattern cantilevers out from the wall. Light from the skylight above filters through the custom perforated stair and projects an ever-changing texture of shadow and light onto the walls and floor of the space. A grand entry door marks the threshold into the relatively small home. The 10-foot-high (3-meter-high) door is made of a two-inch stainless steel tube frame and is manoeuvred by a concealed magnetic locking device and hydraulic pivot.

Patrick Tighe Architecture

# MONTEE KARP RESIDENCE

GROUND-FLOOR PLAN    FIRST-FLOOR PLAN    0    15ft

Location **Malibu, California** Area **2200 ft² (205 m²)** Completed **2014** Photography **Art Gray, Bran Arifin**

Located in the Brentwood neighborhood of Los Angeles, this single-family residence takes advantage of a long urban lot, allowing for expansive rear lawn, pool, and guest house.

The home's plan takes the shape of an 'H' with the kitchen and dining room joining the longer geometries of the ground level, and an aluminum louvered glass bridge connecting the two bedroom sections of the first level.

A spacious interior living room adjoins an outdoor living space, complete with exterior dining area, kitchen, bar, grill, and fireplace shaded by western red cedar roof overhangs, which support the master bedroom's terrace above. A heated and illuminated outdoor lounge provides a place to relax and take in views of the pool. Three bedrooms on the upper level, plus a den and office on the lower level, comprise the additional interior spaces of the house.

Green roofs extending from the bedroom terraces invite foliage inside. Black iron-spot brick and cedar-wood ceilings, featured on both the exterior and interior, further unify indoor and outdoor space. In addition, a material palette of gray acrylic plaster and weathered wood siding anchors the guest house to the main residence.

Marmol Radziner

# MORENO

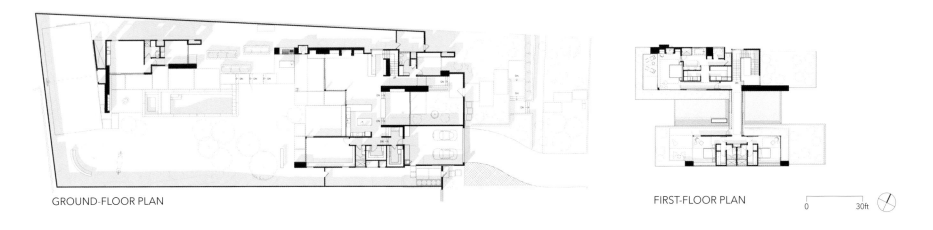

GROUND-FLOOR PLAN

FIRST-FLOOR PLAN

0          30ft

Location **Los Angeles, California** Area **6000 ft² (557 m²)** Completed **2014** Photography **Roger Davies**

Set on a golf course in the Pacific Palisades neighborhood of Los Angeles, this home is a combination of modern and traditional tastes. Zoning restrictions and dual design preferences challenged the architects to find a delicate balance. Mainly, the local homeowners association specified that only 10 percent of the roofline could be flat, a general contradiction to modern architecture.

The design team worked to craft a harmonious home that has a traditional shape yet remains very modern in its detail. The gently pitched roof is complemented with sharp edges and a contemporary slate finish. Additional exterior materials such as smooth-trowel stucco, dark bronze metal and Wisconsin limestone contribute to the clean lines and minimal forms. The home's overall feel is warm and light filled, lending to an atmosphere that is more modern than traditional, without being overly Bauhaus.

The expansive home boasts more than 15,000 square feet of living space. A built-in fireplace warms the outdoor living area, sheltered under a first story sun deck. The patio dining area overlooks a zero-edge pool and cascading landscape, which eventually meets the golf course below.

Abramson Teiger Architects

# NAPOLI RESIDENCE

GROUND-FLOOR PLAN

FIRST-FLOOR PLAN

0       27ft

Location **Pacific Palisades, California** Area **15,000 ft² (1394 m²)** Completed **2013** Photography **Roger Davies**

A warm white primary palette is accentuated with the dark contrast of walnut flooring, paneling, and windows. The layout is open and interconnected, while maintaining intimacy and purpose. The result is a balanced marriage that feels inventive yet timeless.

311

This single-family residence and guest house was designed to broaden the owners' strong emotional connection to the living world. The chosen site, an overgrown man-made pond in an area of the owner's vineyard, was not conducive to cultivation.

In response, the home's design attempts to make the pond and residence a single entity, in which the owners can enjoy and connect with the many types of local wildlife. The building, made of locally sourced Douglas fir and Corten steel, was placed as a bridge across the north end of the pond. The pond itself was enlarged and loosely ordered to integrate with the structure of the residence.

The site plan was choreographed with car parking 150 feet (46 meters) away, granting visitors access to the home only after walking through the forest and across a bridge to the home's main entrance. The broad vista of the pond offers a compressive release upon opening the front door, in the hope of a creating a memorable experience for visitors. Integral to the project's design is the south-facing glazing (Cardinal LoĒ²-272), which maximizes light and warmth in the Pacific Northwest.

Cutler Anderson Architects

# NEWBERG RESIDENCE

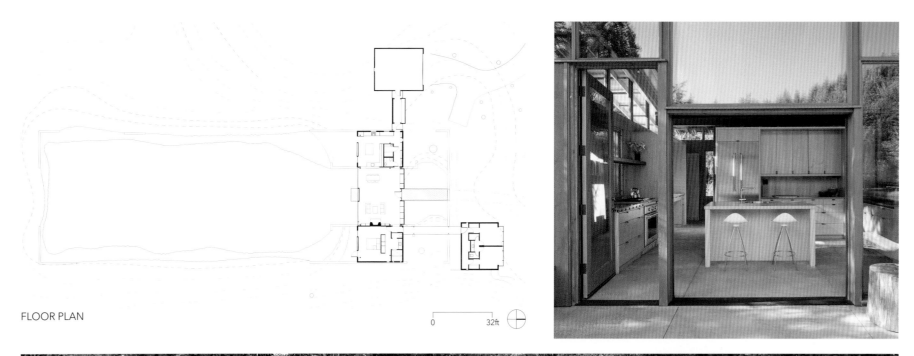

FLOOR PLAN

0        32ft

Location **Newberg, Oregon** Area **1650 ft² (153 m²)** Completed **2014** Photography **Jeremy Bitterman**

Designed as a simple steel frame carrying a wooden roof structure, the primary box houses a kitchen, living/dining room, and master bedroom. An indoor mudroom 'link' connects the home to the garage, while the guest house is connected by an outdoor covered walkway, allowing visitors to fully experience the the site.

This project transformed a 1908 Noe Valley cottage into a cohesive modern dwelling. The home has two distinct faces: one providing privacy from urban street traffic and the other opening to expansive bay views.

Traces of the original cottage are preserved in the massing and circulation of the final building. The grand stair marks the separation between public spaces to the south, and private spaces to the north. The new garage has been incorporated into the public massing, with guest suites both above and below. To the north, the open living area at the heart of the home expands out through a folding window wall to the east-facing deck beyond. Here, residents can bask in the panoramic views of the city and east bay or contemplate the juxtaposition of urbanism and nature in the garden below. Above this main space is the master suite, which takes advantage of even grander views through both framed openings and a lofty private deck. Down below, the owners' sprawling wine collection is nestled into the steeply sloping site in a space with floor-to-ceiling shelving, corked floors for padding, and thermal mass insulation and cooling for consistent climate.

Studio VARA

# NOE

The site had been on the client's radar for many years, admired as he passed by on bicycle rides through the Napa Valley. With an oak-studded knoll, surrounded by four-and-a-half acres of cabernet sauvignon vineyards, the land has an almost archetypal quality–the perfect Napa Valley setting for a beautiful modern wine country home.

In 2011 the property became available and the clients, a couple living in the Silicon Valley area, embarked on their dream home journey.

The design brief was clear. The clients wanted a home that would respect and preserve the beautiful heritage oak trees that dotted the knoll, open up to the beautiful sunsets over Silverado trail to the west, and include generous family outdoor living and entertaining areas oriented to the east side of the property–the quiet side with endless views of vineyards and rolling hills.

The plan has two wings: a north-south wing, which includes two-story kitchen/dining/living spaces, guest suite on the ground floor, and two home offices and a master suite on the upper level. The master suite is located at the north end of the wing and accessed via a dramatic glass bridge, which traverses the double-height great room below.

Swatt | Miers Architects

# OAK KNOLL HOUSE

FIRST-FLOOR PLAN

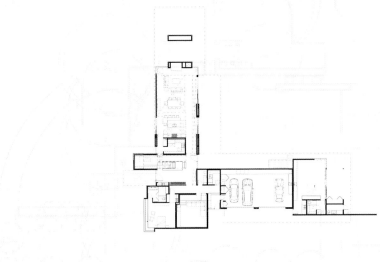

GROUND-FLOOR PLAN

The great room and the master suite enjoy views in three directions. The east-west wing includes the garage and utility spaces, terminating on the east end with a private guest suite. A stone and glass-clad stairway tower, with a unique wine cellar embedded into the landing, forms a vertical anchor in the architectural composition from which the wings radiate.

One of the major themes of this design involves the relationship between architecture and nature. The master bedroom suite emphasizes this dialogue as it cantilevers over a stone plinth and soars into the canopy of one of the beautiful heritage trees, never quite touching the branches. As the branches twist and turn under and over the cantilevered terrace, it's as if the home has always been there, in perfect harmony with its natural setting.

322

Location **Napa Valley, California** Area **5478 ft² (509 m²)** Completed **2016** Photography **Russell Abraham**

Prior to embarking on the design for their new home, the owner chose to live in the existing house for a year in order to gain a holistic understanding of views, sun paths, shade, and how they would best use the property.

The original structure was configured as a linear single-story, glass-and-metal box carved down to basement level at both ends. This provided below-grade access to a garage at one end, and a small courtyard for two lower-level bedrooms at the other. The structural intervention addresses a series of programmatic issues with architectural moments.

The language of simple wood and glass elements offers a recognizable contrast to the aluminum skin of the existing building, and begins to warm the material palette.

A new wood 'tube' was added to bisect the main structure, creating an entry plinth a few steps above the existing floor, and setting up a visual alignment with a new pool house structure across the property.

Blaze Makoid Architecture

# OLD ORCHARD LANE

Set on a hilltop in Atherton this unique home is accessed via a winding drive. Once inside, views in all directions begin to unfold, with the entry canopy framing the distant San Francisco skyline.

Two L-shaped bars balance on top of each other creating courts and overhangs, defining indoor and outdoor spaces with bridges and cantilevers. The home's services are solid elements, which comb the space with walls of mechanism and storage, floating within the open lines of the bars.

The basement is for family play and casual entertaining, opening to a large grassed area below. A light court carved into the ground illuminates the other side of the L. The home's main level has been designed for formal entertaining and cantilevers over the basement, looking toward the city view. Dining, kitchen, and family areas are in the other leg of the L, with stairs leading up the bedroom L, which is inverted and floating above. The leg facing the city is the master suite and is cantilevered over the wing below, creating an outdoor room. In the remaining leg of the home are four children's suites, connected by an office, sitting area, and laundry. They also bridge a void below, which connects to the garages.

Stanley Saitowitz | Natoma Architects Inc.

# OZ HOUSE

The home is a reduced expression of sheer material and absolute form, where connections and intersections are minimized to non-existence.

The building threads and weaves, creating illusionary intersections of space. The bars twist and fold, cross and loop, bridge and divide. At the intersections are vertical connections. These abstract geologies do not impose, but expose, expanding the realm of space and diminishing the role of form. The home's design is largely concerned with transparency and lightness, contrasted with solidity and masses that fold in on themselves, slipping and sliding through space as they frame and connect.

LOWER-FLOOR PLAN

GROUND-FLOOR PLAN

FIRST-FLOOR PLAN

0          40ft

Location **Atherton, California** Area **17,000 ft² (1579 m²)** Completed **2017** Photography **Bruce Damonte**

This Tiburon residence is a classic and inspiring abode that embodies the contemporary through its clean lines and modern design. Located on an east-facing bluff of the peninsula, this secluded, two-story home looks out onto San Francisco Bay. Designed to accommodate visiting friends and a multi-generational family environment, it offers a harmonious balance between private spaces for relaxing and public spaces for entertaining and communal activities.

The entire site was utilized to develop the feeling of a compound rather than a stand-alone building. In order to maximize the natural beauty and foliage surrounding the property, the architects implemented horizontal architecture, which integrates the home into the terraced landscape. Deep overhangs further minimize the structure's height and help elongate its horizontal shape, while asymmetrical window and door arrangements highlight the modern aspects of the residence and provide a rhythm underneath the unifying roof.

Walker Warner Architects

# PARADISE

Although the property sits on a steep slope, the architects were able to create a gracious and inviting entry, as well as fluid indoor to outdoor connections from all main living spaces. The main entrance sits a half-level below the upper level and is complete with broad stairs, a sunken garden, and compelling red door. Unconventionally, this upper level includes an auto court and family entrance, while all living spaces expand across the ground floor and flow easily out to the pool and lawn.

The unique design of the residence derives from the clients' appreciation for art. Their tastes have been translated into bold architectural components, which convey the element of surprise throughout unexpected spaces. Interior designer, Nicole Hollis of NICOLEHOLLIS Interior Design, took cues from the clients' worldly sophistication, minimalist sensibilities, and the site's unique location to craft a wholly integrated and intensely personal interior environment, which connects seamlessly with the stunning architecture and landscape.

Location **Tiburon, California** Area **10,500 ft² (975 m²)** Completed **2015** Photography **Laure Joliet**

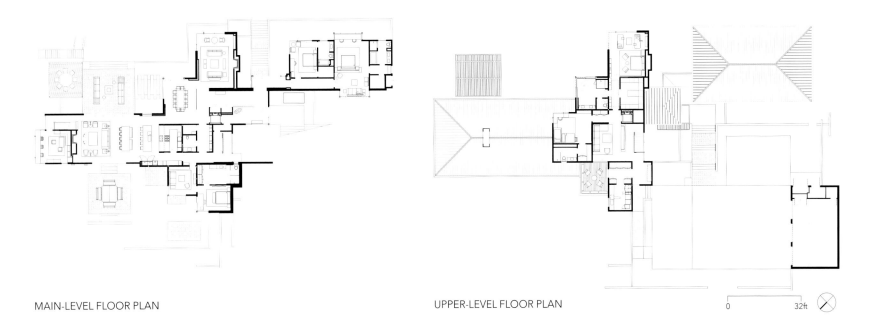

MAIN-LEVEL FLOOR PLAN

UPPER-LEVEL FLOOR PLAN

0          32ft

Sitting on a rocky granite cliff overlooking the Atlantic Ocean, this home is a series of angled glass and raw concrete pavilions, which capture the dramatic landscape in each direction. Crowned by gently curving zinc roofs, each pavilion frames views of a historic lighthouse.

Set along a linear entry hallway, the pavilions also define programmatic areas, with the den, kitchen, master bedroom, and living/dining rooms each ensconced in their own space. On the first-floor, two additional bedrooms cantilever off the main body of the house, further enhancing the experience of the site.

The house is set on landscaped terraces, which provide a platform for lounging areas. Opening out to views with long outdoor patios, these areas recall the deck of a cruise ship. The crashing of waves and wild rocks are a sublime site, creating the perfect balance between architecture and nature.

Alexander Gorlin Architects

# PASHOS HOUSE

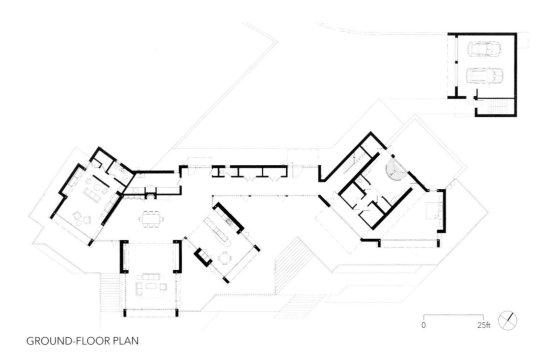

GROUND-FLOOR PLAN

0      25ft

Location **Maine** Area **5000 ft² (1524 m²)** Completed **2015** Photography **Peter Aaron/OTTO**

Located on an exisiting 280-acre (113-hectare) site, in a meadow on the edge of a hedgerow, this home is a contemporary take on a four-bedroom farmhouse. The project was designed with a low surface area-to-volume ratio in order to save costs and simultaneously reflect the simple white form of the practical farmhouse architecture of the region.

Care was taken to minimize disturbance to the land so as to preserve its natural state, including old rock walls found throughout the property. The stone used at the base of the house is Pennsylvania bluestone/fieldstone.

The two-story rolling sunshades were designed to respond to solar gain through the south-facing windows, while allowing excellent daylighting and enabling the building to be safely closed for periods of time when the owners are absent. When the sunshades are closed on hot days the inside temperature is reduced by as much as 20 degrees Farenheit.

Heat is provided via a ground-source radiant heating system, backed up with a wood-fired boiler. The wood for the boiler is collected from deadfall in the surrounding woodlands. A tertiary back-up heating system is provided by the wood stove, which circulates warm air throughout the structure.

The house is prewired for a future solar array to be installed on the white metal roof.

Cutler Anderson Architects

# PENNSYLVANIA FARMHOUSE

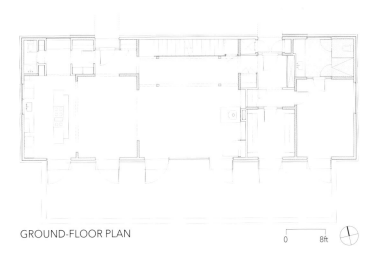

GROUND-FLOOR PLAN

0    8ft

Location **Lakewood, Pennsylvania** Area **4600 ft² (427 m²)** Completed **2016** Photography **David Sundberg/Esto**

This home was designed for an empty-nester couple who, after spending most of their professional lives in Boston, New York, and Chicago, decided to move back to Wisconsin's Door County peninsula. The program asked for a small, unassuming home; a building with an attitude of sincere diffidence to the forest surrounding it. In response, the architects designed a compact structure quietly nestled in a small clearing at the western edge of the gently sloping site, its low-slung silhouette virtually disappearing in the forest's dense vegetation.

The home's rectangular building mass is a tapered space where forced perspective converges at the glazed vestibule, and continues into a recessed covered outdoor room on the opposite side, framing views through the house and into the site's landscape. A continuous wall of milled lumber, stacked at slight angles and finished with a lustrous varnish, creates a highly tactile surface of folding ribbons, and extends from the forecourt into the house, visually anchoring the entry sequence. Inside, the vestibule connects to an open living space, with an oversized sliding-glass door system providing access to a linear patio. Across from the large sliding doors, a delicate sculptural steel staircase, supported by a filigree of vertical rods, anchors the living space and leads to the upper-bedroom suite and the expansive vegetated roof covering the main building volume.

Johnsen Schmaling Architects

# PLEATED HOUSE

GROUND-FLOOR PLAN

0       15ft

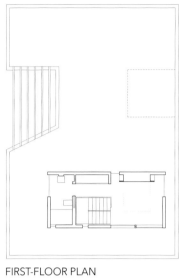

FIRST-FLOOR PLAN

Location **Door County, Wisconsin** Area **1840 ft²** (**170 m²**) Completed **2015** Photography **John J. Macaulay**

The building is clad in charred cedar boards. The boards have been treated using a century-old finishing process known in Japan as *shou sugi ban*. The process of charring is a natural preservative, which extends the life of the siding up to eighty years, reliably protecting the material against rot, rain, insects, and fire. Contrasting the building's dark exterior shell, the interior material palette is dominated by white walls, white lacquered cabinets, and a gray polished-concrete floor.

Located in the historic Prospect Heights District of Brooklyn, this late 19th-century structure was suffering from old age and a general lack of upkeep. In order to convert the weary building into a modern, single-family home, the architect completed a gut renovation, which included the addition of a garden-level rental unit. Many details of the original home were salvaged, restored, and integrated into the new home's contemporary aesthetic.

As a result of strategically placed skylights and an interior light well, the home enjoys sunlight in almost every corner. The wood floor in the stair hall, typically the darkest space in a row house, was replaced with walkable glass panels, transforming the space into a tower that diffuses light rather than absorbing it. The effect is replicated from the parlor floor up, terminating in a ceiling punched with two skylights, specifically designed to bounce light down into the spaces below. The master bathroom is illuminated by the interior light well, which spans two stories up to the roof. A sunroom extension benefits from direct southern exposure through a restored bay window and new skylight.

In addition to their taste for modern architecture, the owners wanted a home that was also environmentally friendly. To help reduce the carbon footprint, a new green roof was installed at the extension, in addition to a 4.5 kW solar PV array at the main roof. This system reduces the electrical load by up to 80 percent over the course of the year.

CWB Architects

# PROSPECT HEIGHTS SOLAR

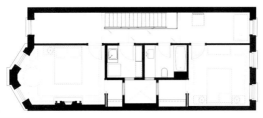

THIRD-FLOOR PLAN

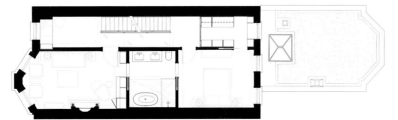

SECOND-FLOOR PLAN

FIRST-FLOOR PLAN

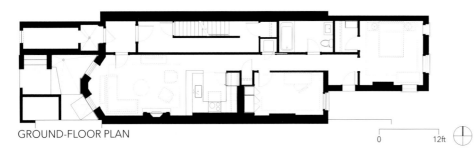

GROUND-FLOOR PLAN

0        12ft

Location **Brooklyn, New York** Area **Main: 3400 ft² (316 m²) Apartment: 1226 ft² (114 m²)** Completed **2012** Photography **Francis Dzikowski/OTTO**

Retrospect Vineyards has been producing and selling pinot noir grapes for 15 years. When the new owners bought the property in 2010 they decided to become more involved in the winemaking process, embarking on a journey to create a new and modern home for their family, along with a working barn and staging area for their annual harvest.

Located on a gently sloping knoll surrounded by 20 acres (8 hectares) of pinot noir vineyards, the home has been designed to provide casual indoor/outdoor living spaces, taking full advantage of the magnificent wine country site.

Oriented on the site with business operations on one side and an expansive view of the surrounding vineyards on the other, the building has been designed with two distinct façade treatments on either side of the narrow T-shaped plan. To the north, a relatively opaque entry court provides privacy and admits daylight through a delicate vertical wood-screen wall, while the south façade eschews solid walls in favor of double-height glazing.

Swatt | Miers Architects

# RETROSPECT VINEYARDS HOUSE

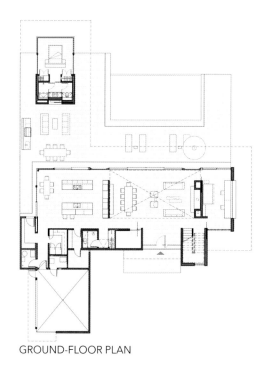

GROUND-FLOOR PLAN

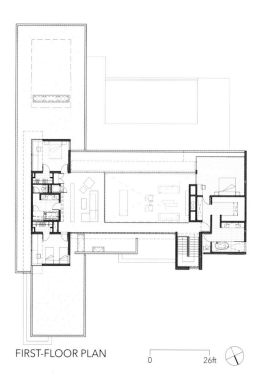

FIRST-FLOOR PLAN

0      26ft

Bedrooms are located above, and public and shared areas below, where a double-height great room occupies the majority of the lower level. On the ground level, the kitchen, office, and great room all open up to a St. Tropez limestone pool terrace. In the great room, sliding glass doors spanning 21 feet (6 meters), seamlessly extend the living space to the outdoors.

The detached guest suite is envisioned as a glass box, projecting beyond the terrace edge and just large enough to enclose a custom freestanding platform bed. While the guest suite functions as a separate building, it remains connected to the main house by a low roof spanning between the two structures. The guest space is screened from the main building and enjoys unobstructed 270-degree views of the landscape. The interstitial space between the structures acts as shaded lanai, with an outdoor kitchen, and vineyard views on two sides.

358

Location **Windsor, California** Area **4986 ft² (463 m²)** Completed **2014** Photography **Marion Brenner, Russell Abraham**

Set on a steeply sloped, east-facing site with long-distance views of the Santa Clara Valley and eastern foothills, this project is a collaborative effort between architect and builder.

The main portion of the home is sited at the top of a knoll and facetted in plan to reflect the topography of the hillside below. It steps down the slope, with roof terraces above and interior living/entertainment spaces below. Exterior living spaces, such as the pool and pool terrace, guesthouse, and outdoor dining are situated on terraced yards further down the slope.

The client wanted a home that appeared to grow out of the land, with warm materials and color palette. The materials include: natural stone veneer, slate roofing, copper details, large sliding, and lift-and-slide doors.

A small but precious collection of vintage automobiles has been integrated into the home's interior experience as a main feature in the lower-level entertainment area. The client wanted the use of lower-level indoor and outdoor areas to emit a resort-like feel. To achieve this, the space is an abstract and simple architectural expression, distinct from that of the main house.

Mark English Architects

# RIDGECREST RESIDENCE

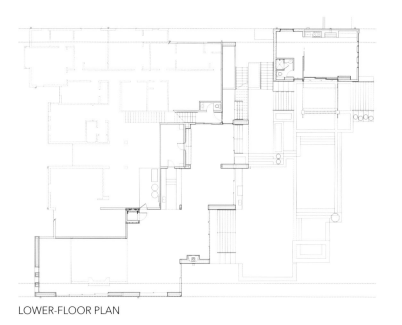

LOWER-FLOOR PLAN

MAIN-FLOOR PLAN

0       16ft

Location **Monte Sereno, California** Area **6286 ft² (1916 m²)** Completed **2013** Photography **Eric Zepeda**

This T-shaped structure responds to the unique typography of the bluff upon which it is situated. At the edge of a cliff, the house sits above a naturally formed wash way, straddling two sides of a stable outcropping of tough, slow-cooled volcanic basalt. The name 'rimrock' refers to this type of geological occurrence: a sheer rock wall at the upper edge of a plateau or canyon. The seam below the house is a natural, preexisting path for animals, which remains unimpeded as they move between the mountains and river. The sensitive nature of the landscape as well as its unique climatic, solar, and seasonal conditions called for careful consideration of materials and positioning of the home.

With the knowledge that changing wind patterns in the winter can create massive snow drifts, hovering the house above the ground plane allows the use of full-height windows to maximize 180-degree views overlooking Riverside State Park and North Spokane, without piles of snow accumulating directly against them.

Olson Kundig

# RIMROCK

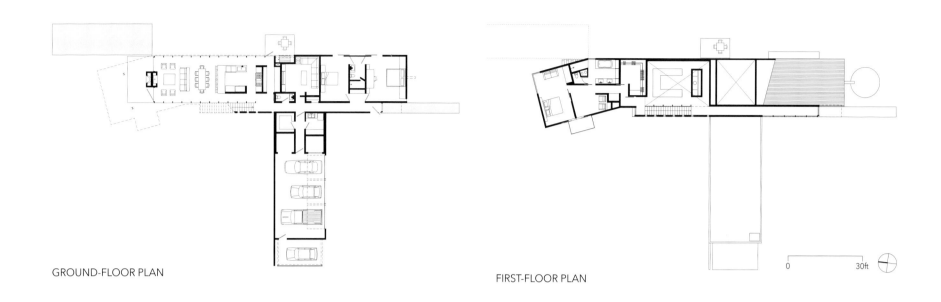

GROUND-FLOOR PLAN

FIRST-FLOOR PLAN

0        30ft

The design reverses the typical transparency one might expect in a home with a large amount of glazing. The upper portion of the building, which is typically most transparent, is actually more private. The lower portion—the public family/gathering area—has more transparency and contains a bridge element spanning the game path. This transparent main level, which consists of the kitchen, dining, and living area, mediates between the prospect and refuge at the edge of the cliff.

The upper part of the house is the most private and is less transparent, with views directed towards tighter vistas. A sense of intimacy throughout the home allows residents to retreat from what is a spectacular yet also aggressive environment.

Tough, durable building materials, mostly mild steel and glass, were used to stand up to harsh environmental conditions and will weather naturally. The steel paneling and structure are reclaimed material locally sourced by the owner. There are automatic, seasonally adjusted exterior shades on all windows, which significantly decrease the energy used for cooling. Erosion on the site is prevented by collecting all rainwater runoff from the roof into dry well, which percolates the water slowly back into the groundwater system.

Location **Spokane, Washington** Area **5200 ft² (483 m²)** Completed **2014**
Photography **Benjamin Benschneider, Kevin Scott /Olson Kundig**

Located on a 350-acre, river-fronted ranch in South Texas, Rio Estancia has been designed for a retired couple and their visiting extended families. Taking inspiration from the panoramic vistas offered on the property, the main home, bedrooms, and guest quarters have been organized in the South American 'Estancia' style to utilize the framing elements of pavilion living. The framed main courtyard and pool are surrounded by mature oak trees, and edge up to the Guadalupe River.

The entry courtyard of the family compound offers a unique natural front door, allowing a full vista of the land. The building program was organized into four zones, offering owners and guests' private areas for living and entertaining as well as privacy and screening for parking. This prevents the interruption of private landscape areas.

The transparent and open plan is complemented with large covered terraces and arbors, extending the living spaces outdoors. Locally quarried stonewalls block north wind, while large southern overhangs control the summer sun. Building orientation, electronically controlled window/mechanical systems, geothermal heating/cooling systems, tankless water heaters, expanded foam insulation, reclaimed water systems, and solar collection have been embraced to create harmony with the climate.

Craig McMahon Architects

# RIO ESTANCIA

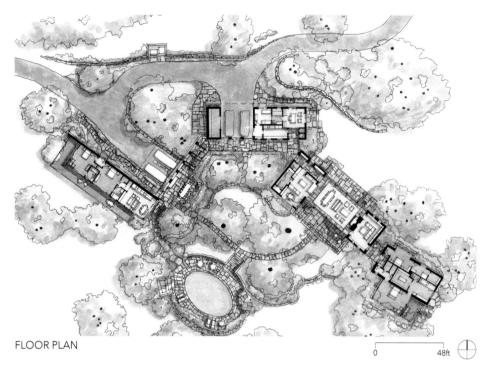

FLOOR PLAN

0    48ft

Location **Kendall County, Texas** Area **7075 ft² (657 m²)** Completed **2012** Photography **Dror Baldinger**

Perched on a hill overlooking a remarkable valley, with Frederick Church's *Olana* in the distance, this 1761 Dutch stone farmhouse was restored after peeling back years of vinyl and Formica-clad additions. The hidden jewel was transformed into a weekend home for New Yorkers, while the farm and original barns were maintained on the property. The significant age of the original colonial farmhouse is obvious. Iron tie rods that hold the roof together spell out 1761, the year it was built.

A great room was created in the house by removing the attic floor to open up the ceiling and expose original oak beams. This space comprises a generous living and dining area. Views of the river valley and the nearby Catskill Mountains unfold through large windows in thick stone walls. All structural additions have been kept to one side, deferring attention to the stone farmhouse and maintaining the intimate scale of the original house. These additions are clad in red siding and corrugated steel panels, establishing continuity with the neighboring farm structures. It appears as if the house was built over time, one pavilion after another.

Alexander Gorlin Architects

# RUTKOW HOUSE

374

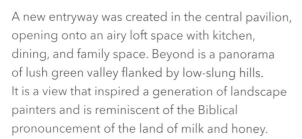

A new entryway was created in the central pavilion, opening onto an airy loft space with kitchen, dining, and family space. Beyond is a panorama of lush green valley flanked by low-slung hills. It is a view that inspired a generation of landscape painters and is reminiscent of the Biblical pronouncement of the land of milk and honey.

From the valley looking up at the house, it appears as if nothing has changed, and indeed that was the intention, a timeless combination of old and new, coexisting in perfect harmony.

Location **Hudson Valley, New York** Area **4500 ft² (1372 m²)** Completed **2015** Photography **Peter Aaron/OTTO**

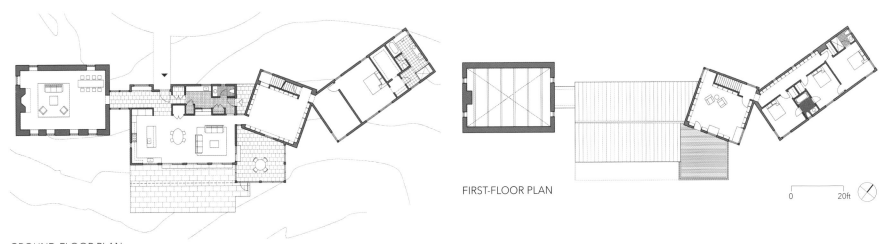

GROUND-FLOOR PLAN

FIRST-FLOOR PLAN

0        20ft

This suburban retreat embraces the street and provides an amplified perception of space on a typical 50-by-150-foot (15-by-46-meter) lot by organizing expansive views throughout the house.

A barn-shaped roof was achieved by tracing the maximum permitted planning envelope, producing a rural reference that fits both the family's background and interest in the informal, modest, and communal. Upstairs, bedrooms open around a lounge area with backlit pegboard that provides a nighttime glow. A Quaker bonnet, seen in an old family portrait, inspired the shape of the guesthouse roof, which backdrops a series of indoor and outdoor spaces. Movable privacy/sun-control screens between house and yard modify views inside and out at different times of day.

Sustainable choices made for the coastal California environment include: drought-tolerant planting, onsite water management, passive shading, cross ventilation, photovoltaic panels, and radiant heating. Materials include glass, concrete, pegboard, drywall, wood shingles, ipe wood, stucco, and cellular polycarbonate.

Koning Eizenberg Architect

# SEE-THROUGH HOUSE

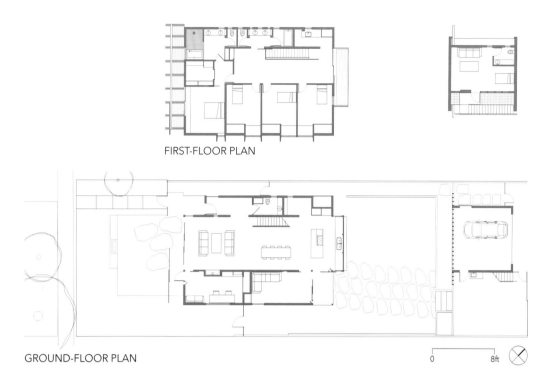

FIRST-FLOOR PLAN

GROUND-FLOOR PLAN

0          8ft

Location **Santa Monica, California** Area **3100 ft² (945 m²)** Completed **2015** Photography **Eric Staudenmaier**

Set among sweeping redwoods and oaks, this Silicon Valley residence embodies a casual California lifestyle through strong indoor/outdoor connections. Harkening back to the property's agrarian history as a walnut orchard, the architect worked closely with the landscape architect to retain the existing redwood and oak trees, and to cultivate an olive grove at the lower half of the site.

The timeless design pulls forms and materials from 80 years of contemporary Northern California architecture, intentionally leaving the specific year of its provenance ambiguous. Cedar walls, exposed framing, and concrete elements can be found both inside and outside. A generous south-facing covered porch faces the swimming pool. The house is shaped like an 'H,' creating two courts that lend all rooms multiple exposures and connections to the landscape.

Another important design move was preserving a 100 year-old, aboveground concrete cistern—a remnant of the site's history. The house subtly refers to the cistern with concrete elements, including a generous staircase that gracefully connects the olive grove and guesthouse to the pool deck and main house. An additional exterior staircase seamlessly links the exterior dining area with the landscape.

Malcolm Davis Architecture

# SILICON VALLEY

FLOOR PLAN

0          16ft

Sustainability was an important consideration to both the client and the design team. Instead of demolishing the original house, the design team opted to carefully dismantle the home in order to salvage lumber and other materials, which were then repurposed back into the home. Time-proven passive-solar concepts were also incorporated into the design, such as southern exposures, thermal mass, cross ventilation for natural cooling, and carefully calibrated solar shading with generous southern overhangs. Other sustainable features include a graywater recycling system as well as photovoltaic panels, which produce electricity and heat to both the domestic hot water and pool.

The residence portrays striking, modern architectural tones, while also offering a tranquil presence against its Northern California backdrop.

Square House is a home with no front or back door, no formal entry, no windows. Instead, all openings as doors. The house has been conceived as a square plan that reinforces its non-hierarchical and unique and informal organization approach. The series of rooms are accessed directly from outside, creating a totally fluid relationship between indoors and outdoors and engaging the landscape through its apertures.

The house is focused on two primary experiences: bathing and rest. A Japanese *ryokan*-style bath, with wooden soaking tub and steam shower are located on the western side of the building. Rest and relaxation occur in and around a sunken, cushioned living room anchored by a large, cast-concrete fireplace. Enclosing this central living area are two small bedrooms and bathrooms, which boast direct access to the outside. The material approach of the project maximizes the sculptural and textural opportunities of cast concrete, allowing the building to sit *in* the landscape as an integrated part of its site.

LEVENBETTS

# SQUARE HOUSE

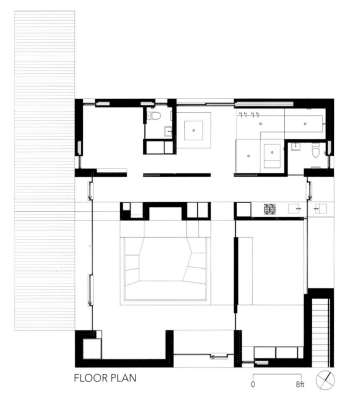

FLOOR PLAN

0    8ft

The sustainable approach to the project is non-technological. Hot water radiant heating, cast into the concrete slab, and large fireplace heat the entire home, while no air-conditioning means very little energy use. With thick concrete walls and floors, and a large self-shaded expanse of southern glass, the house employs passive thermal mass heating. With doors at each room, it can be easily cooled through cross ventilation, reducing carbon footprint and returning to a 'back-to-basics, back-to-nature' principle of living.

Located in a ponderosa pine forest in the Arizona Highlands, this project is a contextual response to the special demands and qualities of a beautiful yet fragile environment. Taking its inspiration from the shape of a pinecone on its side, the design of the cabin embodies both the culture and nature of the forested highland region.

The cabin is nestled in a group of trees on a slope overlooking a small meadow. A faceted geometry recalls a primary house form while also responding to the slope of the land, allowing the cabin to simultaneously merge with and emerge from its surrounding context.

Fire is an integral part of the ecology of the forest, providing a natural way to thin out the forest, reducing the competition for access to sunlight, water, and minerals in the soil as well as allowing trees to thrive. The structure's walls and roof are wrapped in rusted metal siding to resist the effects of wind-blown embers, the color of which is similar to the bark of the surrounding trees.

Studio Ma

# STARLIGHT CABIN

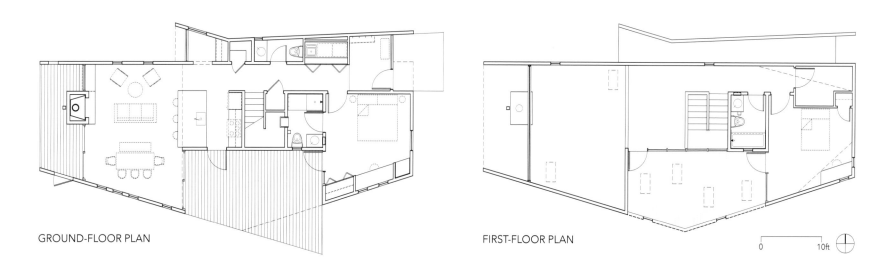

GROUND-FLOOR PLAN

FIRST-FLOOR PLAN

0          10ft

Location **Payson, Arizona** Area **1600 ft² (149 m²)** Completed **2015** Photography **Bill Timmerman Photography 2017**

A compact, energy-efficient design features a centrally located kitchen, double-height living space, and three porches, allowing each living space to be connected directly to the outdoors. This is an important feature considering the region's bright summers, punctuated afternoon monsoons, and snowy winters, and allows residents to experience the outdoors in a variety of settings and orientations without damaging the fragile forest understory. Interior walls and ceilings are faced in stained plywood paneling, the vertical joints of which are covered with wood battens, echoing the standing-seam pattern of the rusted metal cladding.

The result is a cabin that recalls the form and materials of early pioneer dwellings, while also responding to the unique qualities of the surrounding forested landscape. It is a place to observe and participate in the unfolding of ever-changing seasons.

Taghkanic House is located on a spectacular 140 acres (57 hectares) of land in Columbia County, New York. The scale of the surrounding landscape required careful consideration and a master plan for the positioning of structures in order to maintain the site's rugged and rural beauty.

The plan included a main house, guest house, large shed (for land maintenance equipment), vegetable garden, and dipping pool. Conceptually, the whole project and the main house have been designed as a collection of volumes—a modern reinterpretation of the farm structures and barn/storage sheds present on the surrounding farmlands. Just like the old farm structures, the home's volumes are abstract sculptural forms with walls slanted to simulate swaying barns on the brink of falling down. The space and gap between each volume and structure creates an intimate setting, similar to the farm settings nearby.

Hariri & Hariri Architecture

# TAGHKANIC HOUSE

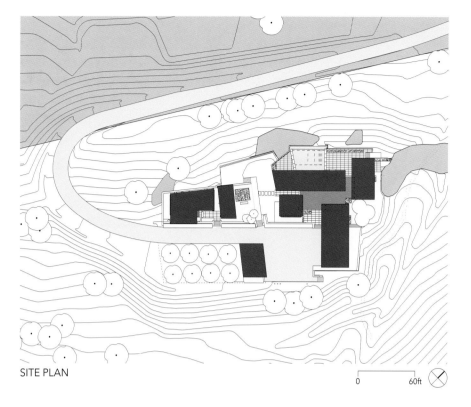

SITE PLAN

0 _____ 60ft

Integration into the land's contours, engagement of the rock croppings, and use of green technology make this country home a refreshing getaway from New York City. Installed like works of art into the landscape, 13 large solar panels provide the home with electricity, while deep geothermal wells assist with heating and cooling. All mechanical components of the house are monitored by a computer, which reports back to the owner around the clock. The alarm system, temperature, shades, and lighting are also controlled by the owner at the touch of a button.

The use of sustainable materials, green design, and cutting-edge technologies, combined with simple, pod-like structures wrapped in ipe wood make this house a unique and cleverly designed country escape.

Sited adjacent to a neighborhood park and overlooking a greenbelt, Turnberry Residence—although largely influenced by the country houses and gardens of England—finds true local expression through its materiality, a combination of Texas limestone, tiled roofing and white oak timber framing and panelling.

Alluding to the more formal aspects of the site and adjacent community park, the octagonal timber-frame library and cut-stone dining room are extensions of the home's public face, both standing proud as pavilions in the refined landscape.

The principle living spaces align along the home's main axis, connecting the entry, library, living room, and kitchen through cut-stone wainscot, timber ceilings, and oak-panelled, plaster walls. The main living space opens to a terraced court created around a mot of live oaks, with views into the greenbelt framed by the master bedroom and service wings. Within this natural landscape, the lower terrace's open-air pavilion focuses on the pool and fountains, overlooking the rustic gardens and creek.

Michael G. Imber, Architects

# TURNBERRY RESIDENCE

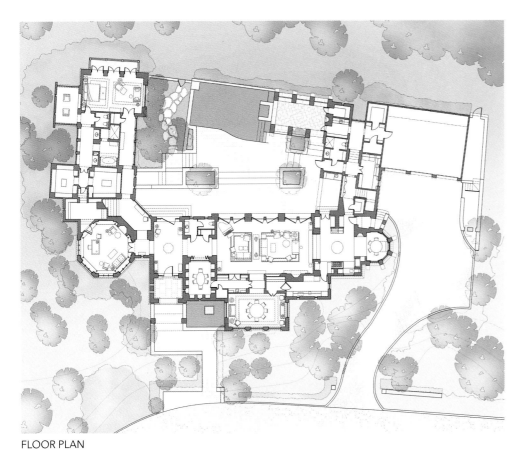

FLOOR PLAN

Location **San Antonio, Texas** Area **10,264 ft² (954 m²)** Completed **2012** Photography **Casey Dunn**

Along the south shore of Whidbey Island lies a stretch of wide, sandy beach, perfect for summer getaways. For decades the clients and their extended family have visited the area. This project recognizes that tradition and celebrates the place itself.

The program called for a single home that would function as two beach cabins combined: one for the owners and the other for guests. In response, the plan provides for two private sleeping wings, flanking a large central gathering space. Each bedroom wing comes complete with its own loft and dedicated water views. The great room, situated between them, has been arranged symmetrically, with identical fireplaces at each end, allowing furniture to be moved seasonally to take advantage of changing light and views. Adjacent to the great room is a communal galley kitchen where family and friends gather to cook. At the beach side, this gathering space opens up to a two-tiered deck, framing a private view of Puget Sound.

Hoedemaker Pfeiffer

# USELESS BAY

The home's design addresses some unusual practical considerations, with frequent harsh weather and heavy use informing virtually all design decisions. A concrete-pile foundation raises the entire structure above the ground to allow storm water to pass freely beneath. Windows, doors, and rooflines have been strategically organized to allow for natural ventilation on warm, sunny days, while also providing the owners with protection from high winds and sea spray. Material selections such as zinc roofing, concrete floors, and solid brass interior fixtures, all share a durable purpose.

This home was designed to be hardwearing but also warm and welcoming, combining the look and feel of a well-worn boathouse with all the luxuries of home. It was built to last and to age with grace.

Location **Whidbey Island, Seattle** Area **4170 ft² (387 m²)** Completed **2016** Photography **Andrew Giammarco**

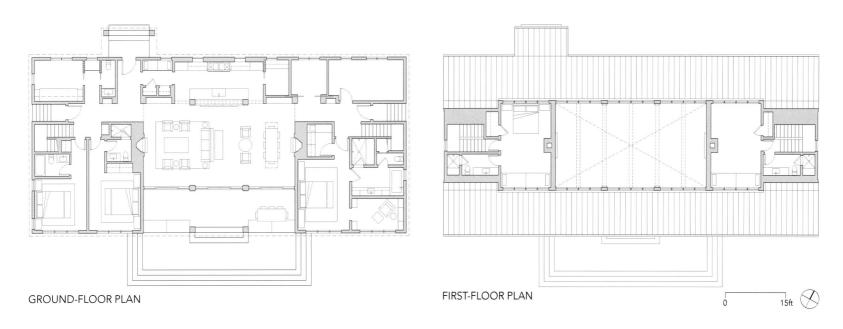

GROUND-FLOOR PLAN

FIRST-FLOOR PLAN

0   15ft

This distinctive residence was envisioned as a piece of inhabitable art for its owner, an avid collector of colorful and unique works. The design features three stepped-back stories linked by a grand mahogany staircase and a double-height glass pavilion overlooking the semi-rural landscape on three sides.

The client had contemplated building her dream house for years before finding the perfect site in Portola Valley, a semi-rural enclave south of San Francisco. The site is a beautiful, gently sloping parcel, with an array of mature oak, cedar, and pine trees providing privacy from neighboring houses yet open enough to afford beautiful views of the landscape. Her design requirements included open planning for interior spaces, zoning of functions to provide a clear separation between public and private spaces, maximization of San Francisco views to the north, and a strong relationship between building and landscape.

The resulting design is based on an L-shaped plan, anchored by a three-story, linear, cast-in-place concrete wall, which projects into the landscape to frame outdoor spaces on both sides of the house. Main public functions are housed on the lower level, while the master suite and a home office are located on the floors above. The short leg includes a one-story home office, detached garage, and guesthouse.

Swatt | Miers Architects

# VIDALAKIS HOUSE

Located on a forest site, this renovated home—unofficially credited to Frank Lloyd Wright—is a weekend getaway and future retirement retreat for a couple living in Evanston. After visiting the remarkably interesting but somewhat understated project, it was hard to imagine it as anybody else's work. The site itself reminded the owners of a verse from one of Longfellow's poem, *Tale of Acadia,* in which the first line reads, 'This is the forest primeval. The murmuring pines and the hemlocks.'

The home's construction was divided into four phases. The first included two wings: an open living space for sleeping and working, and a separate sauna wing including a mechanical room and passageway, which defines the entry connection to the forest beyond. The second phase included the addition of an office and guest room in the sauna wing, and the third, an outdoor shower and fireplace. The fourth and final phase included a private, elevated master bedroom. The same wood finishes continue from exterior to interior, tying all sections of the home together.

Salmela Architects

# VILLIBUNK

412 Location **Door County, Wisconsin** Area **2366 ft² (220 m²)** Completed **2015** Photography **Paul Crosby**

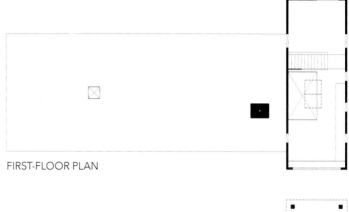

FIRST-FLOOR PLAN

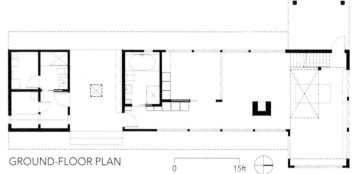

GROUND-FLOOR PLAN
0            15ft

The name Villibunk comes from combining 'villi,' a common homemade Finnish-Swedish yoghurt with 'bunk,' a simplified spelling of a Swedish word for 'pot,' and was inspired by one of the owner's fond childhood memories. She is Swedish-American and the other is English-American, hence the Longfellow verse. Villibunk, as a result, is a personal tale, blending cultures and design.

This project was designed as a family vacation home on a site in Chilmark, adjacent to an agricultural area and with distant views of the Atlantic Ocean. The site was limited because of a unique deed restriction, which set the maximum height of the structure at 6 feet (2 meters) above grade, on the uphill side of the building. The design responded to this restriction by sinking the upper floor into the grade along its north side, and stepping the two floors of the house down the existing slope.

At first, the clients imagined a house that embraced the vernacular forms and materials of the island. However, once the architects started working with the building envelope restrictions, the clients became convinced that a contemporary architectural form would best suit their needs and aesthetic sensibilities, while addressing the unique hillside site.

To capture the view of the ocean and surrounding landscape, a roof deck was set within a flat, planted roof. This strategy preserved the view sheds of properties further up the hill.

Charles Rose Architects

# VINEYARD FARM HOUSE

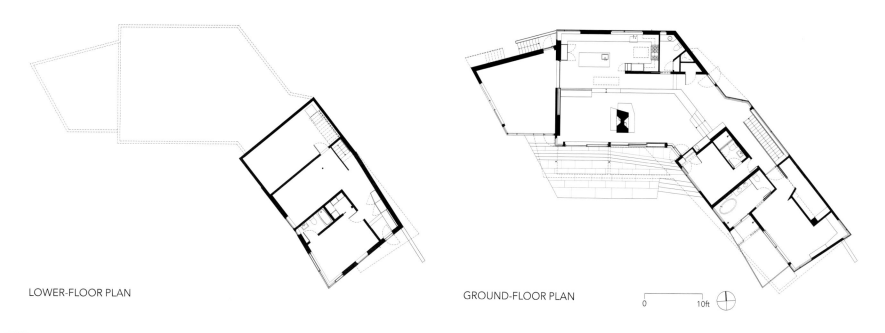

LOWER-FLOOR PLAN

GROUND-FLOOR PLAN

0        10ft

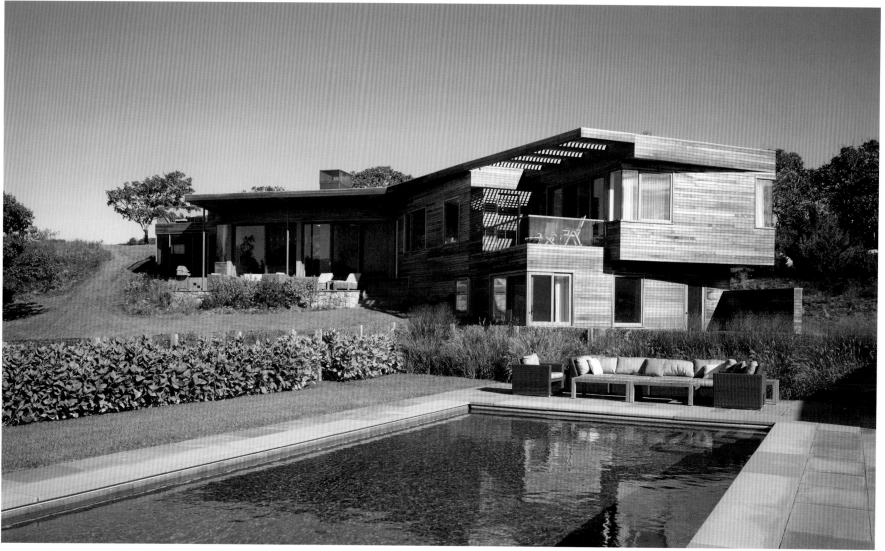

Location **Martha's Vineyard, Massachusetts** Area **4428 ft² (411 m²)** Completed **2014** Photography **John Linden**

The immediate site, distant views, and the quality of light and shadow are at the core of the design. The building's angular shapes and overhangs are responsive to the form of the land and the need for interior shading to reduce glare and create a luminous interior. Multiple terraces, including the roof, offer a variety of vantage points and places to gather as a family. Cedar shiplap, a material that links the building with its historic context, clads the exterior. The interior is a mix of wood, metal, and stone: white-washed, wide-plank white oak; limestone; granite; walnut; and tile.

Extensively remodeled, this home's front courtyard has been defined by elements of fire and water. Upon entry through the theatrically designed entrance, lined with rock fire torches, the home opens up into a retreat of comfort and elegance, with the kitchen, living room, master bedroom, and bathroom all designed as transitional interior spaces. The existing home's interesting forms and design elements provided the architects with an opportunity to transform an existing outdoor space into a piano room, situated off the dining and living area. Curvilinear forms and materials create a backdrop of wood, which provides hidden storage as well as a console with shelving to display artwork. It also helps soften the transition to the hallway.

The wood ceiling and large soffits of the original master bedroom made it feel quite heavy. In an attempt to lift the space the architect pocketed doors behind the television element and opened the room to an outdoor spa and patio area. A fireplace was also added, creating a luxurious place to unwind.

Willetts Design & Associates, Kristi Hanson Architects

# VINTAGE CLUB RETREAT

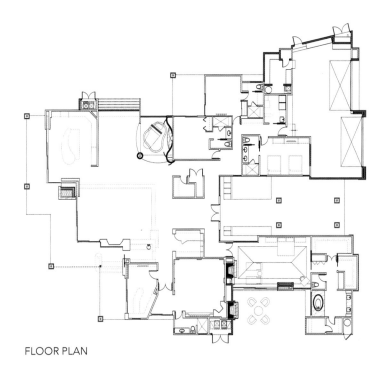

FLOOR PLAN

The home's architectural elements employ organic shapes and reflective surfaces.

Ceilings and soffits in custom-painted silver, gold, and champagne tones add luminous shine complemented by large-scale Cambria floor tiles, all of which work together to reflect the beautiful desert light.

Further additions to the home include a custom wine room and theatre, while the outdoor spa and relaxed seated area, adjacent to the master suite, were existing spaces redone to align with the new home's aesthetic. The kitchen was also completely updated to take full advantage of the indoor/outdoor California lifestyle.

Location **Indian Wells, California** Area **4915 ft² (457 m²)** Completed **2016** Photography **Gibeon Photography, Taylor Sherill**

421

The architects reanimated this 1910 wood-frame row house, suffering from more than 100 years of wear and tear, and updated it for use as a single-family home. The exterior was buried beneath layers of vinyl and aluminum siding, while the inside had been damaged by years of landlord modifications and a fire, which was evident on the underlying wood structure. As a result, every part of the house was rebuilt in a complete renovation. In order for the building to slip inconspicuously into the Williamsburg streetscape, the original wood cornice, which had been hidden under siding for decades, was reinstalled on the new façade.

Inside, the aesthetic provides a warm and neutral base, with pops of color and whimsy throughout the house provided by furnishings, rugs, and drapery. Reclaimed wood flooring, refined oak millwork, and colorful patterned tile play off one another. The décor, provided by Brooklyn-based interior designer Jesse Parris-Lamb, is an eclectic mix of mid twentieth-century classics, exquisite fabrics, and antique treasures sourced from India. The open living space of the ground floor is connected to the family room on the first floor above by a central two-story millwork piece. Beginning as the kitchen pantry, the millwork transforms into a stack of bookshelves, following the path of the stairs to the floors above and anchoring the adjacent spaces to a path of circulation.

CWB Architects

# WILD IN WILLIAMSBURG

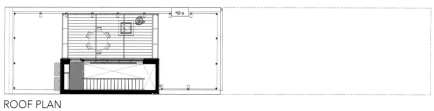

ROOF PLAN

SECOND-FLOOR PLAN

FIRST-FLOOR PLAN

GROUND-FLOOR PLAN

0          13ft

Location **Williamsburg, New York** Area **2800 ft² (258 m²)** Completed **2014** Photography **Rachael Stollar**

The ground-floor living room opens to the landscaped rear yard through a set of oversized sliding doors, providing an area for warm-weather dining. The roof is accessed through a bulkhead clad in weathering steel panels, and shaded by a lightweight steel and cedar pergola covered in vines. The lush rooftop overflows during the summer with vegetables and provides an intimate hangout space. The architects collaborated with Alive Structures on the green roof and back garden.

Located in Calistoga, a small town in Northern California's Napa Valley, this renovated farmhouse sits gently in a landscape of grape vines and matured walnut trees. The clients, who are local winemakers, desired a modern dwelling that would complement their small estate, while working within the structure of the former residence. The home's new design simplifies its relationship to site and ambiguity of the plan through subtle shifts, openings, partitions, and the addition of key unifying elements.

While the previous residence and its newly renovated form share a similar programmatic layout, the inhabitant experience has been reimagined through clear definitions of public and private space. The main entry has been shifted to the center axis of the home, guiding people directly into the open living room and dining area. A cedar-clad utility spine reinforces this articulated boundary and guides views through the home's main communal space.

Bohlin Cywinski Jackson

# WINE COUNTRY FARMHOUSE

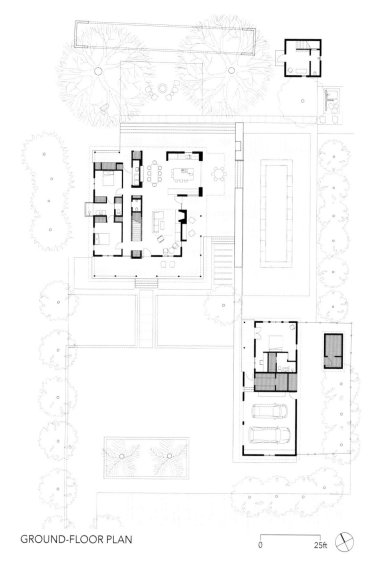

GROUND-FLOOR PLAN

0       25ft

Location **Calistoga, California** Area **4430 ft² (412 m²)** Completed **2016** Photography **Matthew Millman**

The use of cedar siding throughout the renovated portions of the home helps to define the interventions and accentuate the traditional gray-painted cedar shake, punched windows, and white trim of the former design. This same wood detailing is repeated in the cladding of the expanded kitchen volume, which takes on new prominence as the hub of the house and gateway to an expanded deck, rectilinear pool, guesthouse, and renovated water tower. The yard includes numerous opportunities for entertaining, including a built-in barbecue, fire pit, and bocce ball court. Openings at the home's exterior envelope have been increased with the addition of large operable windows and sliding glass doors leading out to a wrap-around porch. Deep overhangs of the hipped roof help shade these areas during the hottest times of the year and buffer interiors from direct solar gain. Enlarged window openings and new skylights provide significant day lighting throughout the house, decreasing the need for supplemental lighting. Preexisting incandescent lights were replaced with LED fixtures, reducing electrical demands, while the addition of solar panels on the roof of the detached garage are expected to further offset the resultant power usage.

The extensive redesign of this dated farmhouse turned modern residence, with its many connections to the surrounding landscape, creates a contemporary home for the clients to enjoy for many years to come.

# INDEX OF ARCHITECTS